Greek Aesthetic Theory

GREEK
AESTHETIC THEORY

*A Study of Callistic and Aesthetic Concepts
in the Works of Plato and Aristotle*

by J. G. Warry

METHUEN & CO LTD
36 Essex Street London WC2

First published in 1962
© 1962 by J. G. Warry
Printed in Great Britain by
Richard Clay & Co Ltd, Bungay, Suffolk
Catalogue No. 2/2536/10

Foreword

This book was originally planned for the benefit of students in Alexandria who had received a French education and found it difficult to understand the different conventions which are often assumed by English literature and criticism. In search of a common cultural ancestor I turned to Aristotle, and Aristotle could not be understood without reference to Plato.

At a later period my work underwent considerable changes and I was fortunate enough to have the opportunity of consulting Professor P. T. Stevens and Professor T. B. L. Webster, to whose advice I am very much indebted – though they should not, of course, be held responsible for any views expressed in these pages.

In its present form the book still adheres closely to its original purpose – that of a Classical background for students of Modern Subjects. For the purpose of interpreting Greek texts I have found it convenient to make my own translations, and at points where the search for concise English idiom has inevitably carried me some distance from the Greek, or where my proposed rendering might not in all quarters command automatic assent, I have added a more literal translation in brackets. This is a simple safeguard which has seemed necessary to me in only a few instances.

J. G. W.

To

the other members of my household

who have in various ways helped

Contents

	Introduction	*page* 1
I	Romantic Beauty in Plato	15
II	The Sense of Harmony	32
III	Plato's Evaluation of Art and Poetry	52
IV	The Poetic Process	68
V	Aristotle on Art and Beauty	83
VI	Mimesis and Rhythm	100
VII	Catharsis	119
VIII	Comedy	136
	Conclusion	149
	Bibliography	153
	Index	163

Introduction

In planning the present work I have borne in mind that most useful things serve more than one purpose, and my purposes here are two. Firstly, it is hoped to give an informative and well-ordered account of aesthetic and callistic concepts as they occur in the works of Plato and Aristotle. This, I believe, may be of advantage to students of modern literature, since the questions raised by the ancient philosophers have in so many instances been rallying points for aesthetic debate and critical theory ever since. To recognize the source of long-discussed and much-elaborated ideas must in itself be beneficial. Much modern thought proves itself, on analysis, to be concerned with the resolution of very ancient dilemmas, and we shall understand the modern thinker better by realizing what these dilemmas are and confronting them, as it were, in their most simple and primitive form. Secondly, my object is, at a time when the value of classical studies is questioned by some educationists, to demonstrate how ancient aesthetics should not be thought of in isolation but boldly applied to present-day problems. I wish to present Greek notions of art and beauty not merely as primitive steps in the advance towards modern ideas but as requiring further investigation for their own sake, like an ancient mine which has not been thoroughly exploited. My classification of material, therefore, will be aimed not only at producing an easily memorable arrangement for the student who wishes to equip himself with information but in exhibiting the theses and antitheses implied in the brilliant but often jumbled or scattered observations which represent the Greek contribution in this domain.

The actual field of my discussion is limited designedly to the works of Plato and Aristotle; for while these two thinkers present us with a striking contrast on which scholars and critics continue to comment, contrast always implies similarity as well as difference, and there is, in these two great philosophers, a profound similarity which unites them and proves many of their differences to be complementary aspects of an essentially similar viewpoint. This similarity – not mere chronology – sets them far apart from later writers like Plotinus or Longinus, both of whom are nearer in outlook to a modern aesthetician than to a Greek thinker of the fourth century B.C. In reading the treatises of later Greek writers, especially those who wrote under the Roman Empire, one cannot help feeling that for them, as for so many critics of modern times, art had become a substitute for life; and indeed, if it was not a substitute for life, what purpose could it have? Neither Plato nor Aristotle had ever successfully answered this question, but neither of them ever regarded art as a legitimate substitute for life. Their staunch refusal to do so is the basis of the claim which I make for them: namely, that together they represent a single school of callistic and aesthetic philosophy.

When I say "callistic and aesthetic" philosophy I in fact underline the point just made. Hegel explains in the Introduction to his *Lectures on Aesthetics* that the term "aesthetic" had at his time already come – however unjustifiably – to apply to the study of fine art, whereas "callistics" is a more suitable name for the study of beauty in general. Hegel was of course interested mainly in aesthetics so defined. The subject of beauty in Nature is dealt with in a comparatively brief chapter of his work, and indeed Natural beauty was for him inferior to artistic beauty. For the fourth-century Greeks, beauty and art were subjects of a different order and could not compare in degree. There was no question of artistic beauty being an improvement on natural beauty, any more than there was of its being a poor substitute for natural beauty. When Plato condemns art as a substitute for life he does so not because it seems to him to usurp life's beauty but because he felt that it usurped life's truth and life's morals, perverting both. This attitude, though not justifiable in the uncompromising terms in which he has expressed it, nevertheless offers a sharp contrast and corrective to the modern view which contemplates art only in terms of beauty. We may also pause to observe that, of the two philosophers whom we are considering, Plato is concerned mainly with beauty (callistic) while Aristotle contributes the study of art (aesthetic). Plato tends to be prejudiced when he writes of art, and Aristotle at the mention of beauty usually turns away with an illuminating but brief and unelaborated observation. The fact, however, that we may identify one of these illustrious Greek names with callistic and the other with aesthetic assists memorable classifications and gives strength to a basic antithesis.

We shall therefore deal with Plato first, not only because he is chronologically prior to Aristotle, but also because the sense of beauty is more primitive and fundamental than the appreciation of art. At this point, for the modern student whose previous first-hand knowledge of Plato is slight, a few preliminary remarks seem desirable. The great majority of Plato's works are in dialogue form, and of these the majority again feature the character of Socrates. Although of course Socrates was a real historical character who won both the love and the hatred of his contemporaries by his habits of "provocative thought", it is not possible to say how far the Platonic dialogues were based on conversations that had actually occurred in Socrates' lifetime. It seems certain that the later dialogues were the product of Plato's own thought – in much of which Socrates would not have concurred. There is no precise agreement on the order in which the dialogues were written, but scholars agree for instance that the *Laws* were written last and that the short and inconclusive dialogues which give us some of the most vivid impressions of Socrates' personality were early. Plato was not by any means the only Greek writer to make Socrates his hero. Apart from the rather blurred picture of Socrates afforded us by Xenophon's *Memorabilia* there were many other writers of Socratic dialogues. Some of these works were imitations of Plato's, but it must also be remembered that Plato himself was not the inventor of the Socratic dialogue. It is generally felt, however, that the portrait which Plato gives us, at any rate in his earlier work, is as faithful to the life as we can hope to discover.

The personality of Socrates was, moreover, an essential stimulus to Plato's literary and philosophic imagination, affording as it did an embodiment of virtues which seem unreal when described in abstract philosophical terms. The metaphysician's need for a hero is perhaps a fundamental religious impulse. The great teacher-hero is frequently a speaker rather than a writer, and Plato upheld the value of the spoken as against the written word; for the biographer of the teacher-hero is usually self-effacing. We may compare the Evangelists and St Paul in their attitude towards Jesus, or Abu Bakr, who assembled the scattered promulgations of Mohammed to form the *Koran*. In a minor way, Boswell's idolatry of Dr Johnson may even belong to the same category. In contemplating the perfection of divinity it is all too easy to lose a necessary sense of personality. Personality is necessary, since only personality can be the object of love, and the need to love, in spite of human imperfection, is one of the main reasons for belief in God. Since, however, personality cannot be conceived in any but human form, it becomes imperative to associate divine perfection very closely with an exceptional and outstanding human personality. Christian Trinitarian dogma affords the most precise expression of this universal religious impulse, and although the Moslems decry it as a profanation of God's perfection the *Koran* frequently refers to the will of God and Mohammed almost as if it were a single will. Here also the association between divine infinitude and human personality is close. Mere perfection cannot become the object of love.

Plato, then, is not a systematic philosopher. He is a dramatist and a biographer fired by religious zeal, and the fact that he was such makes it all the harder to extract the system which is often implicit, though seldom fully expressed, in his work. System is also obscured by his habit of tackling questions of truth and logic concurrently. In this, he differs sharply from Aristotle, who devoted a substantial portion of his work to logic, thus creating an "organon" or instrument with which truth might be approached and dissected. Plato, however, invented a new "organon" with almost every new problem which he approached. Thus in the *Protagoras*, although the subject under discussion is the possibility of teaching civic virtue, a large portion of the dialogue seems to be expended in ascertaining whether lecture or debate constitutes the more valuable teaching method. The greater part of the *Republic*, in which Plato describes an ideal polity, is conceived in the first instance as a logical device for the purpose of discovering the nature and function of justice in a single human soul. In the same way that big letters are easier to read than small, so we are told, justice in the community is easier to analyse than justice in the individual. Plato implies that communal justice is identical with personal justice and that by understanding the one we may understand the other. The logical process is one of analogy, a very unreliable one, and its application in this instance would certainly not have been admitted by, say, Machiavelli. When Plato grows tired of logic or loses faith in the logical system of the moment he turns away from reasoned argument and embarks on a religious parable or myth which carries conviction because of the conviction with which it is written and because of the sublime literary style which such moments of conviction inspired in Plato. At other times, however, Plato will push logic to a ruthless conclusion, even though the logical system which he employs is manifestly inadequate. In the *Sophist*, for instance, it is hoped to arrive at a definition of sophistry by a process of dichotomy. Human faculties are divided into two classes and that which it is wished to define assigned to one of these classes. The chosen class is then subdivided and the faculty in question allotted to its appropriate subdivision. The process is repeated many times and the faculty of the sophist – or quack philosopher – is eventually defined in terms of all the classes to which it has been assigned. The sophists were of course Plato's bitter enemies and it is not surprising to find the sophistic faculty at each dichotomy banished to the less creditable category. At the same time the method is far too capricious to have any logical value. Dichotomies of this kind may be made on as many different principles as there are diameters of a circle.

Perhaps Plato's nearest approach to an Aristotelean "organon" – a system of basic assumptions which could be applied to all problems – was his famous Theory of Ideas, according to which many concepts that we should regard as mere abstractions, inseparable from substance, were themselves credited with substantial value and separate existence. This was plausible enough when ideal beauty or goodness came under consideration but was less attractive when applied to the banalities and sordid details of everyday life; for if material phenomena were, as the Theory demanded, adumbrations of eternal truths, then one was required to believe in such Ideas as "eternal dirt and refuse". Plato shows his awareness of this and many other weaknesses of the Theory in his dialogue, the *Parmenides*. In the *Philebus* he announces his intention of forging other logical "weapons", which were presumably meant to replace the Theory of Ideas. Characteristically, he forges his weapons on the battlefield – that is to say in the midst of a difficult discussion as to the relative values of "wisdom" and "pleasure" as ethical guiding principles in life. The result is highly confusing. The "other weapons" are not really new, being merely a revival of old Pythagorean concepts of limited and unlimited being (roughly speaking "entity" and "fluidity"). The logical apparatus of the *Philebus* is not used in any other of Plato's dialogues. Indeed, it suffers from the same defect as does the Theory of Ideas – namely, that the vital distinction between substance and attribute is nowhere made clear. Such clarification had to wait for Aristotle. Admittedly, there are philosophers today who will tell us that Aristotle's notion of substance was chimaeric, that on analysis all so-called substance reveals itself merely as an arbitrary assemblage of attributes. Yet thought without a concept of substance becomes impossible, and even romantic stragglers from the Bergson and D. H. Lawrence generation, only too glad of an excuse for renouncing thought, may now be taunted with an *a posteriori* appeal to the Quantum Theory, which explains physics in terms of irreducible particles, an ultimate substance incapable of further dissection.

It may seem to some readers out of place to have spent even so much time on mere logical considerations in introducing a work concerned professedly with callistics and aesthetics, but it is hoped that the reading of these pages will be accompanied by direct reference to Plato's own writing either in text or translation, and reference may surely be assisted by general observations of this kind. The Dialogues will seem far less tortuous and confusing if it is realized from the outset what an extraordinary mixture of impatient mystic and almost pettifogging logician their author was; and when at length we come to discuss Aristotle it will be of great value if we appreciate at once how completely devoid he was of Plato's visionary feeling for "existential" realities, how much clearer and stronger a logician he was, and how much better than Plato he realized his own limitations.

We are now in a position to examine a Platonic dialogue

which has particular significance for our present inquiry in so far as it is concerned with the same subject as ours, that is to say, Beauty. I refer of course to the *Hippias Major*. There are two dialogues in which Hippias of Elis, the famous sophist, is introduced as a foil to Socrates, the shorter work being known as the *Hippias Minor*. Hippias also makes an appearance in the *Protagoras*, where as usual he supplies Plato's keen sense of the ridiculous with a target for satire. Hippias, as far as we can ascertain, was an honest clean-living man who took pleasure in his worldly success mainly because it had made him a credit to his parents. It is clear that his sense of filial duty and affection was very strong. He was, however, to judge by any intellectual standard, a self-important mediocrity, and Plato judged him by intellectual standards. This was quite fair, since the sophist's pretensions were intellectual. Hippias collected knowledge much as a junior schoolboy collects stamps, and in this pursuit he was highly efficient, since no intelligent thought had ever entered his head to distract him from the occupation.

Some lines above we described a sophist as a "quack philosopher". In Socrates' time, of course, philosophy held no qualifying examination, and it is probable that Socrates would have regarded a qualifying examination in philosophy as the essence of quackery – or at any rate of superficiality. The sophists were free-lance professional teachers and lecturers. To some extent they were all obliged to pose as educationists in order to justify their activities – or "sell their stuff" as Socrates would have thought, if he had thought in English. Yet all sophists were not as superficial as Hippias. The picture which we have of Protagoras, for instance, is that of a dignified academic. If he could not compete in dignity with our modern University professors it was simply because he had not the honour or the opportunity of serving an often ancient and venerable institution such as a modern University; indeed fifth-century Athens did not even boast an organization such as the N.U.T. bent on "raising the status" of the pedagogic profession. Yet fundamentally the sophist's dilemma was that of the modern educationist. The teacher was trying to take the place of the home in an epoch when home and civic discipline were deteriorating. But was the teacher really the "elder and better" of the vivacious and often aristocratic young men who attended his lectures and patronized his activities? To have made such a claim could have been extravagant and dangerous; on the other hand, by not making it he exposed himself to doubt as to whether he practised what he preached. Socrates and Plato persistently voiced such doubts, and in a letter to Dionysius of Syracuse Plato warmly asserted that character was to be formed by the inspiring example of noble comradeship between teacher and learner, not by mere academic studies (*Ep.* VII. 341 c.). Even those among the sophists who were forced to abandon higher moral pretensions and limit their claims to the teaching of logic or rhetoric remained vulnerable to something like the modern sneer that those who can do something do it, those who cannot – teach. Suppose that we ask a teacher: "Do you intend to make your pupils better men than yourself or merely as good?" He may well foresee the rejoinder that he is unqualified to achieve the former result or that he is unambitious if he merely attempts the latter. A fair and creditable answer, however, might lie along these lines: "With the help of my colleagues, I indeed hope to make my pupils better than I am. Though, in isolation, I should not be able to achieve such a result, it is nevertheless accessible to our combined efforts. The Arts teacher encourages them to deliberate on human relations and affairs, the Scientist teaches them to deliberate on inanimate and sub-human existence, and the athletic coach trains them to act promptly and energetically on occasions when deliberation is impossible or undesirable." No such answer, unfortunately, was available to the sophist. So far

B

from working in a collegiate atmosphere, he was essentially a free-lance in open competition with other sophists.
Nor were all sophists gentlemanly academics like Protagoras. Too often they resembled the modern journalist or
television talker in their flair for catchpenny slogans.

Hippias, for all his domestic virtues, appears to have belonged to this class. In the *Hippias Major*, his character is
sharply and deliberately contrasted with that of Socrates.
His pride in the commercial success of his teaching is exhibited against Socrates' contempt for wealth, his pride in
knowledge against Socrates' ironic profession of ignorance,
his rather abject regard for public opinion against Socrates'
independence of it. Even his pleasure in fine footwear is
perhaps alluded to with intended reference to Socrates'
known habit of going barefooted. In this little one-act
comedy or character sketch – for Plato was more of a
dramatist than Bernard Shaw was a philosopher – there is
little room to develop the theme of Beauty with which it
opens. As we have already pointed out, the question at
issue in a Platonic dialogue is often held in abeyance while
purely logical problems are thrashed out, and this accounts
for the inconclusive nature of many of the early dialogues.
In the *Hippias Major* Socrates is attempting in his own
subtle way to give the sophist a lesson in inductive reasoning. Hippias is so stupid that he cannot even grasp the
difference between a definition and an example. Not even
the logical lesson is mastered, and without it we may be
sure that the inquiry into the nature of Beauty cannot go
very far.

Yet the logic of the *Hippias Major*, limited as it is by the
limitations of Hippias' intelligence, has positive value for
our inquiry. For this logic is the valid logic of the inductive
method and its usefulness compares favourably with some
of the more capricious systems employed in other Platonic
dialogues. The inductive method and the definition of universal application were in fact recognized by Aristotle in

his *Metaphysics* as being the two great contributions of Socrates – not Plato – to philosophy. But Socrates, Aristotle goes on to observe, did not turn universals and definitions into separate realities as did the Platonic school. As we have already shown, the chimaeric substantiation of concepts in this way lies at the root of Plato's Theory of Ideas and haunts him still, even where he has discarded the Theory. Logically speaking, Plato represents a step backwards from Socrates, or at any rate a deviation from the straight line between Socrates and Aristotle. The *Hippias Major*, then, is a Socratic rather than a Platonic dialogue, and indeed, until recent years its genuine Platonic authorship was seriously challenged. In it, no universal definition is reached, but the instances from which such a definition must be induced are ably and ingeniously deployed. After all, the very brevity of the work – it occupies thirty-seven pages of the Oxford text – disclaims anything more ambitious.

At this point, just because the *Hippias Major* offers such a valuable starting-point for our discussion, it would be well to make a short summary of the dialogue. The conversation opens with some brief skirmishing in which Hippias, unconscious of Socrates' irony, boasts complacently of his knowledge and the money it has earned him. Socrates then with insidious humility raises the question of beauty, and asks, ostensibly on behalf of a third, unnamed party, for a definition of that quality. Hippias, as we have observed, has had no experience of definitions and offers examples instead. His first suggestion is that beauty is evident in a beautiful maiden. Socrates points out that a beautiful mare and a beautiful lyre are also beautiful. Hippias agrees, but when Socrates wishes to add to these examples a beautiful pot he is inclined to rebel. Even in the sophist's hazy and unphilosophic mind there is a distinction between beauty which is associated with passion and beauty which is the object of mere approval.

Socrates pleads for a highly artistic "pot", a real master-piece of ceramic art. But Hippias, while conceding such an object as beautiful, objects that a pot is not beautiful as compared with a maiden. This gives Socrates the opportunity to add that a beautiful maiden is not to be compared with a beautiful goddess. A maiden compared with a goddess is as a pot compared with a maiden. Other definitions are now attempted. Hippias suggests that gold is always beautiful. But Socrates reminds him that Pheidias' gold and ivory statue of Athena had eyeballs of stone. Why was the statue not all of gold if gold is always beautiful? Hippias admits that gold is only beautiful when appropriate, and Socrates, pressing the point, despite protests against vulgar instances, elicits the admission that a figwood ladle is more appropriate to its work than a gold one, and that it is consequently more beautiful.

Hippias attempts a further "definition" based on moral beauty. It is in all circumstances, he declares, beautiful to possess health, wealth, and reputation, to live long, give honourable burial to one's parents, and ultimately to meet with the same pious treatment at the hands of one's children. This involves him in awkward mythological consequences. Surely, it would not have been beautiful if Achilles, required to choose between death and glory in youth on the one hand and an undistinguished old age on the other, had opted for the latter! And in any case, how could the divinely born or begotten heroes bury their divine and immortal parents? Socrates now begins to lead the argument. Notions of beauty as "useful" or beneficial are both rejected, and the final interesting suggestion envisages beauty as pleasure received through the medium of sight or hearing – a concept to which we shall give close attention at a later stage, for it occurs elsewhere in Plato's writing. We thus find in the *Hippias* the various classes of beauty with which we are ourselves familiar. There is the formal beauty of ceramic art, consequent on arrangements of line and colour, the

idea to which Socrates returns when he speaks of the pleasures of sight and hearing. Functional beauty, which is outraged by the substitution of a gold for a figwood ladle, is
closely related to formal beauty. The basic ingredient is
harmony. In formal beauty, shapes, colours, and sounds are
united on some single principle to make a pattern. According to the British aesthetician, Bernard Bosanquet, unity in
variety was the sole valid aesthetic principle for which the
ancient Greeks could take credit.[1] Bosanquet underesti-
mated the Greeks. However, unity in variety was certainly
a callistic principle of which Greek philosophers from the
earliest times had been acutely conscious, and it must not
be forgotten that we owe to the Pythagoreans our realization of the essentially mathematical nature of musical harmony. Clearly, we owe our sense of functional beauty to the
same feeling for harmony that is stirred by formal beauty;
a diversity of effort and device is co-ordinated by a unifying
purpose, or different purposes are co-ordinated in a single
work with a result which gives greater stimulus to each.
The principle of unity and variety holds good. So it comes
about that formal and functional beauty easily mix, as in
the instance of the beautiful mare cited by Socrates. The
creature might be appreciated as admirably adapted for
some particular human purpose – say, drawing a chariot.
Or the disposition of its limbs and the glossiness of its coat
might in themselves unite to suggest energy, control, and
vitality.

Even when we arrive at personal and moral values, the
sense of harmony – of unity and variety that is to say – perhaps still plays an important part. The beautiful maiden
suggested by Hippias as an obvious example of beauty may
perhaps be judged by the same canons of harmony as a
horse or an artefact. Our appreciation may also be functional. Do we not expect of female beauty that it should

---

[1] Bernard Bosanquet, *A History of Aesthetic*, 1892, Allen and Unwin,
London, reprint 1949.

express the tenderness of motherhood with the liveliness and grace that a man looks for in his consort and companion? And then again – what of Hippias' standards of filial piety and their inherent moral beauty? Surely, here also there is a fittingness, a propriety of behaviour comparable to the propriety of the figwood ladle. Yet Hippias is somehow right in feeling a difference between personal and moral beauty on the one hand and inanimate beauty on the other. He acquiesces uneasily in the examples of a beautiful mare and a beautiful lyre, perhaps because of the exalted human associations which these objects evoke. But even the most magnificent work of pottery, he finds, belongs to a lower order of beauty than the maiden. Socrates' insistence that a beautiful goddess is superior to a beautiful pot is an adequate logical answer to anything that Hippias can say in defence of his own instinctive predilections, but of course the complete inability of Hippias to reduce any sentiment to a thought is the main point of the dialogue. The modern reader must feel very much as Hippias did. The difference between a goddess and a maiden is much smaller than the difference between a maiden and a pot. For even if the modern reader has not had much experience of goddesses, he may nevertheless recall Dante and Beatrice and many other great idealized loves in history and literature. Romantic beauty easily leads us to the sublime, but formal and functional beauty in animals or in inanimate creation seem to belong to another order. The difference surely comes with the advent of personality.

CHAPTER I

Romantic Beauty in Plato

We concluded our introduction with the remark that
beauty seemed to be of two kinds: the formal, intellectual,
functional beauty on the one hand and the passionate,
romantic, and often sublime beauty on the other. This
change of quality appears to be brought about wherever
personality is involved in the beautiful object. At the same
time, we must ask ourselves: are we not, by dividing beauty
in this way, falling into Hippias' error? Beauty is a single
appellation which may reasonably be expected to denote a
single reality. If we divide our reality into two, then in one
case the name must be misapplied, or applied only in virtue
of some casual association; or else in one so-called class of
beauty something has been superadded which does not
exist in the former. Something like this seems to have happened in our argument, for did we not say that beauty was
transformed at the point where it came into contact with
personality? And ought we not then to say that beauty is
the sense of harmony present in personal as in impersonal
beauty, and that romantic or religious passion are stimulated not by beauty but by the personality which happens
to be associated with it? In this case we should go on to
add that our attraction or repulsion by another personality
is not a question of beauty but of goodness, and we should
agree with Bosanquet that when the Greek philosophers
included morality as beautiful "Greek aesthetic unquestionably cast its net too wide". Yet if we probe our
personal experience, some instinct surely calls for the re-
jection of this conclusion. There is a difference between
loving and being in love. We love the good but fall in love

with the beautiful, and this is true not only on the human but on the religious plane. For when we love our neighbours in the manner of the good Samaritan we are following love's discipline, but this is quite distinct from love's vision, which, as the Russian existentialist, Nicolai Berdyaev,[1] points out, is responsible for the more sensational exclamations of many Christian mystics and for a consequent flavour of heresy which often outraged more matter-of-fact theologians. Beauty in personality would thus appear comparable with an intimate chemical compound, not a mere physical mixture, and the fact that it seems to crave a common appellation with the impersonally beautiful argues that it is somehow associated with such impersonal beauty. The association, however, may be profound or casual. If it is casual, then our duty is to break it by the use of distinguishing nomenclature. If on the other hand it is profound we shall know that we have discovered the ingredient or power which exists no less in detached intellectual delight than in ardent personal passion. This ingredient or power will then deserve the name of Beauty.

We are here so close to Plato's thought that it is desirable to turn once more to the study of his writings. For in different passages scattered throughout the Dialogues we find that Plato has in his own quite unsystematic way devoted a great deal of attention both to personal romantic beauty and to the cooler impersonal intellectual beauty. The connexion between the two is not so easy to discover from his writing, so far from that indeed that a critic might well despair of the attempt. Thus Professor R. Hackforth writes in his commentary on the *Philebus*: "He (Plato) approaches Beauty now not from the standpoint of erotic mysticism, but from that of aesthetic analysis. To seek to 'harmonize' these approaches is futile, for Plato's thought resists forcing into a single mould." Yet if the two approaches cannot be har-

---

[1] N. Berdyaev, *Spirit and Reality*, translated by O. F. Clarke, University Press, Glasgow, 1935.

monized it still remains our philosophical responsibility to show where the disharmony lies, not merely to abstain from discussing the matter as Professor Hackforth's note might seem to suggest. Moreover, if we may take the reader into our confidence at this early stage, we must admit to having a secret – a secret belief that the two approaches can be harmonized, and that the evidence for such harmony can be discovered in Plato's own writing, if only one knows where to look!

It would perhaps seem more orderly to begin by considering those passages in Plato which are concerned with impersonal beauty, since this, at any rate in Hippias' scale of values, appears to have been thought of as a lower standard of beauty and from an evolutionary point of view might well be considered as prior to personal beauty. Actually, however, we shall do just the opposite, and our reasons for doing so are as follows. Firstly, the *Symposium*, which better than any other dialogue illustrates Plato's view of romantic beauty, also contains passages which are of consequence when we wish to consider intellectual beauty, so that rather than any other dialogue it should be taken as as basis for comparison between the two. Secondly, a more sustained and systematic account of romantic beauty is given in the *Symposium* than is accorded to any kind of beauty anywhere else in Plato's works. The *Phaedrus* might be considered as a possible rival in this respect, and we shall certainly be right in studying it in connexion with the *Symposium*, but on examination the *Phaedrus* seems to provide us with a more detailed and minute study of what is merely a single stage or aspect of the system in the *Symposium*. The *Symposium* is therefore the more comprehensive authority on the subject and should be taken first. Between them, the *Symposium* and the *Phaedrus* more nearly approach an organized account of romantic beauty than anything which can be assembled from Plato's observations in the corresponding field of intellectual beauty. A solid basis in the former domain may, however, assist and stimulate inference in the latter. Perhaps also, I should apologize for vague terms like "romantic" and "intellectual" – especially "romantic" in connexion with Greek thought – but definition is our goal and not our starting-point, and it is expected that such terms will be familiar to the reader through association. The ability to convey meaning through association is an advantage which the philosopher enjoys over the mathematician. It is only of supreme importance that he should know when his use of words is associative and when terminological, i.e. grounded in definition.

Let us then talk about the *Symposium*. The title of this dialogue is sometimes translated as "The Banquet", but this is to be deplored. "Symposium" only means "a drink together", and although the habit of methodical drinking without solid condiment is observable mainly among northern barbarians, "banquet" is a term unhappily suggestive of Lord Mayors and aldermen, quite inappropriate to the intimate little party which Plato describes. "The Cocktail Party" would probably convey more to a modern reader, except that the Greeks enjoyed their "drink-togethers" sensibly, reclining on couches instead of standing up uncomfortably in a crowded room. The coincidence of title with Mr Eliot's play would then seem hardly an accident, for the theme and mood of the two works is curiously similar. Both works achieve their atmosphere in circumstances of refined conviviality, where an intimate "drink-together" among intellectuals leads to an intimate "talk-together". In both works also the theme is that of sublimated passion – though in the Greek work the emphasis falls on homosexual passion. This may seem distasteful to a modern reader of normal susceptibilities, but to allay any sense of outrage we shall say more on this subject at the end of the present chapter. For the moment it will be enough to insist that sublimation is the essence of Plato's idealism and that the phrase "platonic love", as we have come to understand it, does not disclaim sexual attraction though it precludes sexual activity.

The story of the famous party is told by a man called Apollodorus to his friend some sixteen years after the party itself is supposed to have occurred – for we cannot be absolutely certain how far the occasion was historical and how far a literary prototype based on the actuality of many such parties. Apollodorus had heard the story from Aristodemus, a devoted follower of Socrates, and Aristodemus was apparently "following" Socrates at the time when the narrative opened, for it happened that Agathon, the young tragic dramatist, was celebrating his recent stage success, and Socrates was invited to the celebration. It appears that Socrates took the liberty of bringing Aristodemus along with him and then absent-mindedly forgot where he was going, so that Aristodemus turned up rather embarrassingly in the manner of a gate-crasher at Agathon's house well in advance of the philosopher. Agathon, however, understanding the situation at once, immediately puts the unbidden guest at his ease, and Socrates himself arrives on the scene soon after. Other guests were Phaedrus, a pupil of Hippias, the sophist whom we have already met, Pausanias, a close friend and literary admirer of Agathon, Eryximachus, a medical man, and Aristophanes, the great comic poet, eleven of whose works have been preserved for posterity. Of Agathon's own works nothing has survived, and this is a pity, for in Aristotle's *Poetics* we may find some tantalizingly interesting information concerning his dramatic output. It appears that he wrote tragedies, as a modern dramatist might, with fictional characters and no reference to the traditional themes of Greek tragedy. He was also something of a critical theorist and based his plots on the principle that "it was probable that something would happen contrary to probability". At an epoch like our own, when the best elements in civilization seemed committed to self-destruction, life itself was possibly too tragic to allow any relish of the more poignant forms of stage tragedy, and Agathon's climaxes seemed to have aimed at the grim rather than the pathetic (*Macbeth* rather than *King Lear*). Aristotle blames him for trying to cover too wide a field of action in one of his plays and also for conforming to the later practice of inserting irrelevant choral odes; his importance, however, is beyond dispute and our lack of any extant work from his pen represents a serious gap in our knowledge of Greek drama.

Agathon's party apparently followed an even more bibulous meeting on the previous night, and the fact that some of his guests had barely recovered from the effects of it was responsible for their decision to make it an evening of organized talking rather than organized drinking. Each of them agrees to make a speech in praise of love, and indeed each one of them in his own way is an artist in words, but Socrates, when called on to contribute, insists on analysis rather than eulogy of love's power. Socrates has just time to finish his speech amid general applause when the party is interrupted – and eventually disrupted – by the arrival of an extraordinary drunken character, noisily attended. This is Alcibiades, one of the most "talked of" men in Athens, whose many-sided personality in the course of his life exhibited him to the public imagination successively as playboy, philosophical dilettante, military hero, star of Athenian progressive politics, criminal, traitor, lady-killer, the saviour of his country, and finally the uttermost of "outsiders" that ever have been. Alcibiades throughout his life suffered from very few inhibitions, and on the night when he turned up, gracefully drunk, at Agathon's party to crown the victorious poet with ivy, violets, and ribbons from his own head, he was feeling even less inhibited than usual. In answer to his demand that the company should drink, Eryximachus urges that Alcibiades also should contribute a speech in praise of love. The latter, however, insists on praising not love, but Socrates, and his praise takes the form of a remarkable personal confession such as even he might have blushed to utter in a moment of stark sobriety. Intellectual powers may become the object of physical passion, just as physical beauty may be the object of balanced intellectual appraisal, and it appears that in the days of Alcibiades' adolescence, when his youthful beauty was the sensation and scandal of Athens he had formulated a deliberate plan to captivate and corrupt Socrates. The plan had hopelessly miscarried. Not only had Socrates proved himself quite incorruptible, but he had not even been shaken out of his attitude of benign serenity by the precocious boy's shameless advances. After such a testimony, not surprisingly, organized conversation breaks down and gives way to general drinking. The last thing which Aristodemus remembers is Socrates in argument with Agathon and Aristophanes concerning the respective functions of tragic and comic poetry. By the time that the two playwrights had fallen asleep it was already dawn. Socrates and Aristodemus quietly left the house. The philosopher then had a good wash and went about the day's business.

It is hoped by the foregoing account to convey something of the atmosphere of the *Symposium* to those who have not yet read it; the dialogue, however (it is one of Plato's greatest), owes its organic unity to something more than atmosphere. Socrates' speech, in which love is analysed as the love of beauty, gives summary expression to what is a complete callistic theory, yet the speeches of the previous speakers must not be regarded as irrelevant or simply superseded by Socrates' words. The effect is cumulative. One speech affords a starting-point or debating-point for another; and the final revelation of Alcibiades is designed to show that Socrates is no mere sophist, but is perfectly capable of putting into practice the principles which he has just eloquently expressed. Our present concern, however, is with Socrates' speech in particular. As has been noted, it follows Agathon's and is preceded immediately by a brief interchange between Socrates and Agathon in which the poet is obliged to admit that love is not, as he had dramatically declared, supremely beautiful. For love implies desire, and desire argues a lack of that which is desired; and love which is aimed at beauty and goodness must consequently lack those qualities. Agathon accepts the refutation good-naturedly and Socrates immediately begins to enlarge on the argument.

As usual when putting forward a positive and constructive view, he disclaims knowledge himself and attributes his thesis to a mythical third person. On this occasion he cites as his authority a "wise woman" of Mantinea called Diotima. Mantinea was a town in the north Peloponnese, but the choice of locality is explicable as a punning reference to the Greek word meaning "prophecy". Socrates, also, according to this own account, had once considered love beautiful, but Diotima had disabused him of the idea by the use of such arguments as he had just employed against Agathon. Moreover, it follows that love is not, as Agathon pronounced, a god – for the gods are good and beautiful. At the same time, it is impossible to think of love as ugly, and the conclusion is that love is a "daemon" or spirit, intermediate between the human and the divine. Love is not beauty but the desire for it, just as philosophy is not wisdom but the desire for it. The possession of great qualities begins with a sense of deficiency, and it was Socrates' own modest claim to distinction that he realized better than other men the extent of his own ignorance. However, it becomes necessary to distinguish the love of beauty from the love of the good. All men love what they conceive to be the good in the sense that they desire it; but what is this special passionate desire which we understand by the phenomenon of "being in love"? Diotima explains that he who is in love desires to "beget the good upon the beautiful", and this notion provides the starting-point for a system of education through beauty. Those who are physically in love beget human children in the ordinary way, but it is possible also to be spiritually in love and to beget acts of heroism and self-sacrifice. The desire for beauty and the desire for immortality are closely allied, and while we may perpetuate ourselves instinctively in our offspring in the way that the animals do, the acquisition of an immortal reputation offers a higher and more satisfying means to self-perpetuation. Man's fulfilment of his destiny depends on his power to wean desire from physical objectives and concentrate it upon sublime ambitions, and Plato realized that a homosexual attachment provided an even keener stimulus to such sublimation than did a normal one. Alcibiades' confession and, more particularly, what is said in the *Phaedrus* on the same subject prove that Plato was not blind to the degrading dangers of such attachments, yet at the same time temptation to the perverse is often closely linked with a call to the sublime – simply because the path of mediocrity is closed. Sometimes there is no middle course between heroism and cowardice, sanctity and corruption; and this situation may occur through some crisis or coincidence in life – as it occurred to Joseph Conrad's hero in *Lord Jim* – or it may come about through an ingrained disposition in personal character. Certainly one must admit that an educational system or spiritual "askesis" founded on such situations is an all-or-nothing, a sink-or-swim venture.

So, according to the system ascribed to Diotima, the lover of a handsome boy must turn his attention from the love of one to the love of many such beauties. This, of course, is a step upwards, for the love of many must not be confused with the love of any. The lover of personal beauty wherever it is found cannot hope to become the paramour of personal beauty wherever it is found, and to that extent the physical outlet is dammed and a reservoir of power created for spiritual ascent. From the love of physical beauty in general the lover must now turn his thoughts to beauty of mind and character, and he will of course be helped in this if he can at first discover beauty of mind and body in a single person, but later he is content if chance throws in his way even a poorly endowed young friend whom by his own superior knowledge and experience he is able to help. Here a new factor apparently comes into play, a sense of "strength made perfect in weakness". The emphasis is no longer on contemplation but on conduct. The period of spiritual tumescence has ceased and given place to spiritual procreation. At this point the lover turns away from personal beauty altogether and ardently immerses himself in the activities and laws of civic life, where also he discovers a field of beauty. This exalted passion in turn gives way to study and philosophy where contemplation is closely linked to original thought and output. The final step on the Platonic ladder is taken when the aspirant to immortality perceives Beauty first as a universal quality pervading all creation and secondly as an eternal Idea detachable from it. Here we cannot follow Plato too closely without becoming involved in his controversial Theory of Ideas, but it would seem that in the *Symposium* he envisages a state of beatitude in which virtue has become effortless delight, so spontaneous that there is no distressing period of tension between the tumescence which Beauty excites and the Good which is begotten on Beauty. The shadow no longer falls between "the emotion and the response".

Turning from the *Symposium* to the *Phaedrus* we find that while not co-extensive their themes overlap. Or rather – there is a substantial portion of the *Phaedrus* which can be regarded as an expansion of the erotic philosophy outlined in the *Symposium*. Even this statement needs modifying, for it is only the lower rungs of the spiritual ladder, the stages in which Beauty still adheres to the personal, that receive fuller treatment in the *Phaedrus*. Before commenting, however, we should perhaps place before the reader a few general facts about this other great dialogue. The *Phaedrus*, we must admit at once, is not a well-wrought unity in the manner of the *Symposium*, but rather the contrary, for it falls awkwardly into two halves. Phaedrus himself is of course the speaker of the *Symposium*, Hippias' pupil, and in the course of a country walk with Socrates by the banks of the Ilissus he discusses a rhetorical exercise by the orator Lysias, in which animal passion is paradoxically exalted over romantic ardour. The argument is rather similar to the line of talk adopted by D. H. Lawrence and his school in the thirties. Nature is upheld at the expense of human nature. Civilized impulses are regarded as mere perversions of primitive innocence. Man must return to the animal, not advance to the divine. Challenged to make a similar speech, Socrates launches an attack on romantic love; he has nothing, however, to say in favour of animal appetite, and soon revokes even his denunciation of love. This revocation constitutes the portion of the dialogue with which we are at the moment mainly concerned. When it is finished, the conversation turns once more on the subject of rhetoric in general. What is here said concerning literary values is of considerable interest but of no particular relevance to the foregoing analysis of erotic passion and its sublimation. As we have observed, the dialogue lacks the unity of the *Symposium*, since the discussion of rhetoric and the discussion of love are only very loosely linked by the circumstance that love happens to be the chosen subject of the rhetorical exercise originally submitted for criticism.

Let us, however, consider Socrates' "revocation", for in so far as it takes the form of a eulogy on love one naturally places it beside the similar eulogies of the *Symposium*. It belongs to the "set". In some respects, however, it exhibits a difference of tone from the *Symposium* – a difference which is only faintly adumbrated in Alcibiades' confession towards the end of the latter dialogue. Socrates' speech in the *Symposium* enlarges upon the glorious potentialities of sublimated passion. Indeed, the *Phaedrus* also proclaims the

c

triumph and reward of the pure and noble lover, but at the same time it lays far more stress than does the *Symposium* on the dangers and pitfalls of passion, the spiritual agonies and carnal temptations which beset the lover in his progress. We may compare the treatment of erotic passion in the two dialogues with two aspects of modern psychiatry. Sublimation must be accompanied by suppression. The reservoir is tapped for power only after the uncontrolled torrent has been dammed. Psychiatry has distinguished between "repression" and "suppression". The former denotes the non-recognition of an instinct and constitutes a kind of self-deceit. The latter implies a refusal of immediate outlet to a well-recognized impulse. The superficiality of the journalist often confuses the two processes under the single head of "inhibition". For "suppression" is old-fashioned morality, sublimation a great invention of modern science, and "repression" one of the habits that are supposed to have gone out with Queen Victoria. The journalist of course must always be in fashion. So while he extols sublimation and denounces repression (or "inhibition"), he remains silent on the subject of suppression. He could not possibly recommend anything so out-of-fashion, however commendable. It is hoped, however, that modern students of Plato's theory of beauty will have diluted the muddy concoctions which journalese thought pours willy-nilly down our throats with the clearer draughts of more scholarly and critical reading, and that consequently in turning from the *Symposium* to the *Phaedrus* they will feel that they are doing nothing retrograde, even though the latter dialogue suggests that discipline and self-control and resistance to temptation and other such outmoded concepts play an essential part in spiritual progress.

Socrates' account of love in the *Phaedrus* is elaborated with reference to a parable of fallen nature – literally fallen. For the soul, we learn, once lived with the gods in Heaven, where it was equipped, like the gods, with a two-horse chariot and followed the gods in their career through the firmament to the outer surface of the heavenly vault to feast upon sublime visions of ideal Truth and Beauty visible from that vantage point. But whereas the horses of the gods are equal to their task and eager for it, the human chariot is betrayed by one of the horses on which it is forced to rely, a vicious and refractory brute, unworthy of his noble yoke-mate who responds so well to the prompting of the chariot-eer. So it comes about that human souls never quite attain to the full panorama or to the "Plain of Truth" on which their horses are pastured, and they eventually fall back to earth with nothing but a dim memory of the sublime experience which they once briefly enjoyed, benighted in a world whose phenomena are meaningless save when they serve to fan that memory to a slightly warmer glow. In Heaven, we are told, some souls were more successful than others in following the gods to their glorious vantage point, and in these the memory of divine realities persists more strongly. Such souls become philosophers in their sublunary existence, and less privileged souls become kings, statesmen, business-men, athletes, medical men, religious functionaries, poets or artists, artisans or farmers, sophists or demagogues, and last of all tyrants – in descending order of merit according to the purity of vision which they enjoyed above the heavens.

The myth of course has an important bearing on Plato's theories concerning the transmigration of souls, according to which the intuitive basis of knowledge is explained as recollection of a previous existence. With such theories, however, we are not here concerned, and it is not necessary to follow their development in the *Phaedrus*. What does concern us is the history of those souls which have tumbled to earth, their wings bruised and broken by vain attempts to hold their own in the milling field of charioteers who followed the gods. The fallen soul still retains its original three-fold composition, symbolized by a driver and two horses, one of which is good, the other bad. The soul's recollection of past glories is very dim, but certain semblances of beauty, especially those discovered by the lover in his beloved, remind it so strongly of the original celestial Beauty which it knew before its incarnation in a world of mere semblance, that its crippled and shorn wings are stimulated to fresh growth; and with this growth there occur the growing-pains which are the commonplace of romantic personal relationships. For while the driver, aided by the good horse, is trying to rediscover his heavenly home and to muster such strength and inspiration as will enable him to return to it, his sense of nostalgia is aggravated by the refractory performance of the bad horse which does everything in its power to drag him downwards into animal sensuality. Only philosophers, who enjoyed the clearest vision in their celestial existence and who followed the chariot of Zeus, greatest and wisest of gods, in its career to the zenith, are proof against this treacherous element in their own nature. Those who followed Ares or some slightly lower deity, though capable of noble comradeships, cannot be guaranteed against degrading lapses.

If we wish to compare the accounts of sublimated passion given in the *Symposium* and the *Phaedrus* there are one or two interesting points to be noted. The *Phaedrus* concentrates on that stage in the philosopher-lover's progress in which he is still enamoured of a single person. Sublimation takes place in so far as the power of physical appetite is eventually directed into spiritual channels and harmonized with a lofty sense of beauty; this sublimation, however, is achieved within the framework of single, lifelong, "marriage of true minds". There is no question of progressing from the love of one beautiful body to the appreciation of beauty in many, in the manner prescribed by the *Symposium*. Secondly, there is a suggestion that love is prompted not only by the excitement of spiritual and physical tumescence which seeks to relieve itself in communion with some objective beauty, but

that the lover's sense of beauty is also subjectively determined. For we are told that those who followed Ares in their
heavenly career will tend to seek lovers of "martial" and
forceful character, whereas those who followed Zeus are
more restrained and philosophic. Thirdly, there is a suggestion that Plato did not dissociate his erotic concept of
beauty from his more formal and intellectual callistic notions, such as we have seen foreshadowed in the *Hippias
Major*; for in the *Phaedrus* we are told that beauty is apprehended chiefly by the eye, since this is the clearest of the
senses. It is worth remembering that the word for "seeing"
in Greek is etymologically germane to that which denotes
"knowing", and the same is true in other Indo-European
languages. If pressed to name the second "clearest" sense,
Plato would hardly have done other than name that of
hearing, for after the eye the ear is indisputably the finest
minister to the intellect.

The most important way, however, in which the *Phaedrus*
differs from the *Symposium* is, as we have already indicated,
in its sense of guilt, its almost Christian concept of fallen
nature and original sin as embodied in the symbol of the
vicious horse. As in the *Symposium*, the very essence of the
personal relationship envisaged in the *Phaedrus* is its homosexual nature. Yet here, much more than in the *Symposium*,
is evidence that Plato, himself a homosexual even among
Greeks,[1] considered carnal homosexuality vicious, just as he
considered sublimated homosexuality holy. He also clearly
thought that the spiritual possibilities of such relationships
as he described justified the risks which attended them. A
brief consideration of Plato's attitude towards sex in general
will convince us of the consistency of his outlook. In the
Hippias Major (299 a) we are told that the sexual act presents so repulsive and ugly a sight that it can be performed
only where there are none to witness it. Apart from the ex-
cretory associations of corruption and decomposition, Plato

[1] See *Diogenes Laertius*, III, 291 ff.

would probably have deprecated the act in so far as it is a spasm. In the tenth book of the *Republic* he writes with disgust of the spasms of weeping and laughter, for they are irrational and uncontrolled. This is a view with which it is easy enough to sympathize. A spasm in so far as it is irrational lacks formal beauty, and sexual orgasm is one of the least rational and controlled of all spasms. The act becomes beautiful, however, when it is associated with procreation and birth. These associations not only rationalize it, but enlist it in the cause of immortality; and immortality, according to Plato's argument in the *Symposium*, is the contribution of Beauty to Goodness. Men not only desire what is good but desire that the good should be theirs for ever, and the act of procreation, whether of a sublimated and spiritual order or of the natural and physical order, is also an act of regeneration, renewing life in its products. There is nothing here alien to the modern view. The sexual act, though ugly on the face of it, is rendered beautiful by virtue of its associations with birth, regeneration, and nurture. Deprive it of these associations, and one is left only with the ugliness – as in a homosexual act. We are discussing the purely aesthetic (or callistic, as we should say in deference to the terminology originally adopted) point of view; and though it might be pleaded that the force of such associations is no weaker in a homosexual act than in a heterosexual act of predictable infertility, average sentiment finds in the conjunction of male and female an indispensable symbol if the act is to be redeemed.

Here modern feeling is certainly not at variance with Plato. The modern student, however, may part company from him over the question of sublimated homosexuality, especially when the dangers of such sublimation are admitted – and Plato does in the *Phaedrus* admit them. It would be pretentious to claim a keener and finer moral sense, more easily appalled by risks of this kind. For it can be demonstrated that our objections are not moral. We are not appalled, for instance, by the love of Lancelot for Guinevere or Tristan for Isolda, and we sympathize with Paolo and Francesca as surely as Dante sympathised with them. Indeed, were they not betrayed by an unguarded moment,[1] like the homosexual lovers referred to in the *Phaedrus* (256 c)? Clearly, we are not disgusted by immorality, and an adulterous liaison may impress us as noble even though sinful. It is all too easy to sanction taste as "good" merely because it happens to be one's own. Thus Jowett, in his preface to the *Symposium*, writes: "Nor does Plato feel any repugnance, such as would be felt in modern times, at bringing his great master and hero into connexion with nameless crimes. He is contented with representing him as a saint, who has won the 'Olympian victory' over the temptations of human nature."

Now, Socrates' only "connexion with nameless crimes" was that he resolutely refused to have anything to do with them, and this in spite of a calculated scheme to tempt him. Jowett considered it a glaring fault of taste that Plato should have referred to such an incident. For chronological reasons Jowett was, of course, unacquainted with the theories of Freud and might have maintained that certain offences were better left nameless. Nevertheless, as a clergyman he must have known that temptation does not in itself constitute sin (even if Socrates had felt tempted), and he seems to admit that, on the contrary, temptation overcome is an occasion of merit. One suspects from the passage quoted that Jowett would have been less offended at a heterosexual sin than at a homosexual temptation; and in this he is representative not only of nineteenth-century but of twentieth-century public opinion.

---

[1] Soli eravamo e senza alcun sospetto . . .
  Ma solo un punto fu quel che ci vinse . . .
                              (*Inferno*, V, 129, 133.)

CHAPTER II

The Sense of Harmony

We have entitled this chapter "The Sense of Harmony" with a view to sharpening the contrast between intellectual and romantic notions of beauty. The propriety of the term "romantic" in connexion with Greek thought of the classical period has already seemed to call for comment and apology. It is hoped, however, that the foregoing chapter will have done much to justify the term. Not only has our use of the word "romantic" admitted the popular associations of erotic passion but also the more literary suggestions of emotion accentuated by conflict and nostalgia. So we now undertake to examine Plato's concept of harmonious beauty, fully conscious of the antithesis implied in the ideas of conflict on the one hand and harmony on the other. I would also like to draw the attention of all students of later European literature and critical thought to the pertinence of this inquiry to the great classical-and-romantic antithesis – one might almost say "controversy" – which has dominated our literary and artistic culture for the last three centuries. It is not too much to claim that if we succeed in establishing a synthesis between a notion of beauty apprehended through conflict on the one hand and harmony on the other, we shall have gone far towards reconciling the classical and romantic ideals upon a common basis. In English literature we find the dilemma neatly presented by Jane Austen in *Sense and Sensibility*, where she makes her hero say: "I like a fine prospect, but not on picturesque principles. I do not like crooked, twisted trees. I admire them much more if they are tall, straight, and flourishing. I do not like ruined, tattered cottages. I am not fond of nettles, or thistles, or heath blossoms. I have more pleasure in a snug farmhouse than a watch-tower, and a troop of tidy, happy villagers please me better than the finest banditti in the world." Jane Austen, however, although she tried very hard to be fair, took sides; and if one takes sides in a debate, true synthesis becomes impossible. It is perhaps one of the advantages of classical studies that they enable us to consider our problems, as it were, at arm's length. The ancient Greek and Roman world is sufficiently remote to allow a detached and cool view of matters which have become controversial under the stress of their immediacy. At the same time, the Greco-Roman heritage is first and foremost the birthright of modern Europe, and because of this we are able to identify ourselves with the doubts and aspirations of antiquity in a way which would be quite impossible if we based our literary culture on, say, Chinese or ancient Indian studies. Even the Arab civilization which bloomed so healthily in the eleventh century, mainly owing to Greco-Roman inspiration, was soon to be smothered and sand-choked by the Islamic desert wind.

With such considerations in mind, let us apply ourselves once more to the Platonic dialogues. As we have already suggested, Plato's treatment of intellectual beauty is by no means so systematic or complete as is his development of the romantic approach in the *Symposium* and *Phaedrus*. Consequently, we shall be dealing with passages in which our theme is scantily glanced at, often by way of asides or *obiter dicta*; but for this very reason we shall be able to avail ourselves of one facility which we did not enjoy in the previous chapter. It will be possible to quote the fragmentary material with which we are concerned instead of contenting ourselves with a résumé. Here, in translation, is an important passage from the *Philebus* which strikingly develops the idea already outlined in the *Hippias Major*, namely that Beauty is pleasure through the medium of eye and ear. An attempt is being made to describe pure pleasure, that is to say pleasure which is not marred by the fevered intensity of a deferred satisfaction, or mingled with irritation like that of "scratching". Protarchus asks what pure pleasures are and receives the following answer from Socrates: "They centre in those colours and forms which we describe as beautiful, as well as in odours for the most part and sounds and all those things which are unheeded and painless in their absence, though their presence is felt and fraught with unalloyed pleasure."

The debate is then pursued:

Protarchus: And how, Socrates, can these claim the attributes which we have assigned to them?

Socrates: Well, I suppose that what I have said is far from clear, but I will try to clarify it. By beauty of form I do not mean, as is commonly meant, the creatures of nature and pictorial art. But let us put it like this: I mean straights and curves and all that a lathe, rule, or square may produce from them in plane and solid form. Do you grasp my meaning? These, I maintain, are not instances of relative beauty, like other things, but are eternally and essentially beautiful, conveying their peculiar pleasure, which is utterly dissimilar from the pleasure of scratching. There are, moreover, colours in which the same type of beauty and pleasure is inherent. Do you understand?

Protarchus: I am doing my best, Socrates. Will you please do your best to be clearer.

Socrates: What I mean is this: steady, clear reverberations of sound, emitting a single melodic line which is tonally pure, are beautiful essentially and not in virtue of any external relationship: and the pleasure which attends such beauty enjoys the same kind of independence.

Protarchus: That is so.

Socrates: Odours of course are productive of a less sublime type of pleasure. But any pleasures in which no mixture of necessary pain is inherent, through whatever sense and in whatever substance we encounter them, should in my opinion be classed with those that we have just mentioned. Do you understand?

Protarchus: I do.

Socrates: Then let us also add the pleasures of learning, if we can assume that these contain no element of hunger and that any pre-existing hunger is in such cases painless.

Protarchus: I would agree to that assumption.

Socrates: But consider this: a satiety of learning may be followed by forgetfulness with consequent depletion. Do you still detect no element of pain in such pleasures?

Protarchus: None that is felt instinctively, but reflection on the experience may prove painful in cases where our learning constituted a useful asset and its loss is regretted.

Socrates: Precisely, my good fellow, but we are at the moment concerned only with instinctive experience which is untempered by reflection.

Protarchus: In that case you were right. The forgetting of what we have learned is not a painful process.

Socrates: These pleasures then must be regarded as unmixed with pain, appealing not to the common man but to a very select few.

(*Phil.* 51 b–52 b)

The apprehension of beauty described in the *Philebus* is quite obviously of an intellectual order. Whereas the *Symposium* investigated the relationship of Beauty to Goodness, the foregoing passage is concerned with Beauty in relation to Truth. Our enjoyment of colours, forms, and tones is allied to the pleasure which we take in learning and intellectual activity. According to Socrates' explicit argument the point of similarity resides in the "painlessness" and purity of all such pleasures, but a little reflection will reveal that their "painlessness" is no coincidence, for the enjoyment of colours, forms, and tones is itself essentially intellectual and therefore associated with "learning". Eye and

ear (and, thinks Socrates, sometimes our sense of smell) supply cognition with its units. Elementary perceptions of
colour, form, and tone supply us with those fundamental
notions of kind and degree without which thought is impossible. Seeing and hearing, as long as their objects are
abstract and mathematical and free from any material associations are intellectual pleasures, and such pleasures only
become tainted when the abstract form which gives rise to
them receives some concrete embodiment.

However, the passage which we have quoted from the
Philebus sharply accentuates the contrast between intellectual and romantic beauty, and would seem to make reconciliation between the two concepts, if anything, more
difficult. Intellectual beauty is essentially painless and
effortless, yet romantic beauty, as we saw in the *Symposium*
and *Phaedrus*, is attained after suffering and endurance as a
result of a deliberate application of the will. Yet Plato certainly does not envisage two types of beauty with nothing
but a casual association to justify the common appellation,
for when he tells us that the pleasures of smell are less
sublime than those of sight and sound, we are reminded of
the relationship between beauty and sublimity as it is explained in the *Symposium*. The sublime (literally "the
divine") is that which possesses the characteristics of immortal deity. It is the eternal. We naturally ask: if sublime
and eternal joys are available to the soul in elementary
intellectual pleasure, why should it need to embark on the
arduous spiritual "askesis" outlined in the *Symposium* and
the *Phaedrus*? The answer must be that the epithet "sublime"
admits of comparison. We are told that odours are less
sublime than sights and sounds. Presumably, then, sights
and sounds may be less sublime than other forms of experience, for example, the experiences described in Plato's
accounts of erotic aspiration. To such a supposition, however, an objection at once occurs: the pure pleasures of the
Philebus are superior because they are painless; erotic aspira-

tion is far from painless, and must therefore be inferior. The two approaches to beauty can only be reconciled on something like the following hypothesis:

Both intellectual and romantic sublimity (in its full attainment) represent an unalloyed delight in harmony. The sublimity which is the object of romantic aspiration is higher than an intellectually apprehended sublimity, because the former absorbs the soul's entire experience, whereas the latter is a blessed moment which stirs us to evanescent ardour before it fades. The vision of absolute beauty described in the *Symposium* is, on the contrary, as Plato expressed it, "neither waxing nor waning". To the extent that the effect of intellectual beauty is evanescent it may seem that Plato has wrongly described it as "painless". The mere transience of delight is in itself an occasion of pain. But this point has been anticipated by Socrates when he pleads that learning is a painless pleasure, even though we may lament forgetfulness of what we have learnt. There is no pain inherent in the experience itself as there is in the pleasure of "scratching" or the pleasure of cold water to a fevered throat. If, however, we contrast intellectual beauty not with the beatitude which crowns romantic aspiration in its triumph but with romantic aspiration itself, we realize that such aspiration, mixed as it is with pain and evil, with a sense of guilt and unachieved harmony, is to that extent inferior to the primitive and untainted intuitions of form, colour, and tone. Plato has clearly indicated the relationship between romantic aspiration and ultimate beatitude, but he has not marked so clearly the relation between intellectual beauty and beatitude. We are obliged therefore to deduce that he views the soul as emerging from innocence into the conflict of experience. Here it strives to impose upon experience the formal harmony which it apprehended in innocence and, if it succeeds, attains to a fuller and more permanent bliss of which formal delight was merely a fleeting promise.

For the time being, however, it would be well to leave any further philosophical implications alone and assure ourselves that what is said in the *Philebus* indeed represents Plato's considered opinion on formal beauty. In collating a system from scattered and fragmentary references it is all too easy to take observations out of their context or to give undue weight to *obiter dicta*. Furthermore, we have already noted that Plato, just as he will frequently jettison logic in pursuit of an intuition, will also on occasion doggedly pursue logic for logic's sake in the very teeth of his own fervent belief. In the *Philebus*, which to some extent represents an experiment with a new logical system, it would not be surprising if we arrived at a certain amount of un-Platonic thought. So let us test the callistic views expressed in the dialogue for their Platonism. For the concept of Beauty as pleasure reaching us through eye and ear, we have, of course the support of the *Hippias Major*; but this does not go quite far enough. In the *Philebus* Socrates is made to insist very strongly on the distinction between pure forms and colours on the one hand and the creatures of Nature and pictorial art on the other. The same distinction seems to be implied in his designation of one pure series of musical notes as an unalloyed pleasure. He contemplates such a series of notes in isolation from musical art as an almost mathematical phenomenon. His insistence on the "purity" of melody probably means that there must be no verbal accompaniment, though music without words was, among the Greeks, quite exceptional. In the *Laws*, on the contrary, Plato seems to censure "songs without words" (669 e), but he is here blaming such compositions for their lack of moral content, whereas in the *Philebus* he is thinking of sound as a natural source of pleasure unrelated to artistic composition. The requirement of purity also seems to preclude the distortion of the musical intervals, a common contemporary practice to which Plato apparently objected in any circumstances. He certainly objected to it when it occurred in the course of musical art (*Laws* 655), if indeed we may interpret his reference to "coloured" music as an attack on chromatic or enharmonic usages. In the *Philebus*, *a fortiori*, since his concept of pure pleasure is almost mathematical, any circumstance which blurred the distinction of units would be unacceptable. It is in any case easy to appreciate the parallel between forms and colours which imply no natural object on the one hand and gradations of musical tone which imply no explicit meaning on the other.

In claiming, however, that the passage quoted from the *Philebus* represents Plato's considered view of the subject we expose ourselves to one very pertinent objection, which must be disposed of before we can with clear conscience proceed in our argument. In the *Republic* (476 c) Plato writes: "The devotees of audible and visible pleasure gladly entertain beautiful sounds, colours, and forms and everything which may be created from these. Yet their minds are not capable of perceiving and entertaining the nature of beauty itself." He goes on to stress that few souls only will attain to the apprehension of ideal or sublime beauty. To believe in relative beauty merely "is not to live but to dream", and he whose attitude is dominated by such an inadequate belief makes the mistake of the dreamer. He confounds similarity with identity. We are therefore bound to question whether the beautiful sounds, colours, and forms of *Republic* 476 b are to be identified with the pure colours, forms, and tones of the *Philebus*, for if they are to be so identified the contradiction is glaring and bewildering. The latter are not relative. They are absolute. The sounds, colours, and forms of the *Republic* are given precisely as instances of relative and not absolute beauty. Furthermore, Socrates appends to the above-cited passage in the *Philebus* the remark that the pleasure of learning will recommend itself only to a select few. As the pleasure of learning is associated in the *Philebus* with sounds and colours under the head of "pure pleasure", there appears to be a further discrepancy between this dialogue and the view expressed in the *Republic*, where the select few have risen to spiritual heights which make the pleasures of eye and ear seem no more than feeble adumbrations.

At first sight it may seem tempting to reconcile these two statements by making use of an explanation which we have already given, namely, that the formal pleasures of the *Philebus*, in so far as they are fleeting and momentary – not continuous and eternal like the absolute beauty of the *Symposium* – are in fact relative. Indeed, does not Time render all things relative? Yet when Socrates maintains that the pleasure of learning is not in itself affected by subsequent forgetfulness, he makes it quite clear that he is considering the quality of intellectual pleasure in itself, and leaving its transience out of the question. The time factor is deliberately ignored. In any case it is stated quite uncompromisingly that the formal pleasures of eye and ear are not relative but absolute and sublime. No, the apparent contradiction between the *Philebus* and the *Republic* can be explained without recourse to any philosophic subtleties. The true explanation rests simply on Plato's language, style, and idiom. Surely, in the *Republic*, "beautiful sounds, colours and forms and everything which may be created from these" must be regarded as a species of hendiadys for "everything that is created from beautiful sounds, colours and forms". James Adam, one of the greatest editors of the *Republic*, notes three other examples of such hendiadys in the dialogue (328 c, 429 e, 558 a). None of these is a perfect hendiadys; the one notion underlying the twofold expression is in no instance quite single. Thus Adam's notes describe the three examples respectively as "virtually a hendiadys", "a sort of hendiadys", and "almost a hendiadys". In the first instance, where old Cephalus' couch is depicted ("a sort of pillow-and-couch contraption") the couch and pillow are thought of not quite as a single unit, yet at the same time Plato is aware of them as components, so that they are a way of saying "a pillowed couch". In *Republic* 476 b the form of expression is very similar. Plato is thinking of music and pictures as well as of the sounds, colours, and forms which constitute their components. He is not thinking, as in the *Philebus*, of sounds and colours and forms carefully dissociated from music and art. It should also be noted that, according to Plato's belief, the purity of such sounds and colours would be tainted by the juxtapositions of art, and we may compare his scornful allusions to the type of painting which particularly made use of such juxtapositions (e.g. *Phaedrus* 69 b), perhaps in the manner of modern European impressionism.

Moreover, the cogency of the foregoing observations is enhanced when we recall that the passage in the *Philebus* describing formal beauty employs a type of semi-hendiadys precisely similar to that which we have discovered in *Republic* 476 b. "I mean," says Socrates, "straights and curves and all that a lathe, rule or square may produce from them in plane or solid form." Is this not the equivalent of "all that a lathe, etc., may produce from straights and curves"? The straight and curved forms are not wholly dissociable from the matter which embodies them, for we are here considering the pleasures apprehended through the eye. So far then from there being a confusion, there is a strongly marked antithesis between the pleasures of the eye as described in the *Philebus* and those pleasures which are alluded to in *Republic* 476 b. In this last passage, the phrase which we have translated "everything which may be created from these" certainly includes, even if it is not confined to works of fine and useful art. It might possibly be extended to cover works of natural creation, but could not embrace simple geometrical design. Such design, whether in plane or solid form, would never have been regarded as the outcome of "creation".

Before leaving the question of formal beauty altogether there is another passage in the *Republic* (584 b) which we

D

ought to consider if we are to rescue Plato from suspicion of self-contradiction on this point. Odour is here proposed as an example of "pure pleasure", but we should at once notice that although odour alone is here specified by Plato, he advances it only as one instance among many of the same type. The passage runs as follows:

"Consider the pleasures which are not consequent upon pain, and just see whether in an instance like the following you can possibly regard pain as the loss of pleasure or pleasure as the relief of pain."

"What instances?" he demanded. "What pleasures do you mean?"

"In order that you might grasp my meaning," I said, "I had in mind particularly the pleasures of odour, though many other such pleasures exist."

What, let us ask, are the many other unspecified pleasures of the same type? Surely they can be no other than those enumerated in the *Philebus*. The only question which remains to be answered is: why does Plato here cite the pleasure of odour as characteristic of pure pleasures, when in the *Philebus* its place among them is conceded only on the understanding that it is less sublime, and while in the *Hippias Major* its inclusion among callistic pleasures is openly ridiculed (299 a)? The explanation would seem to be as follows. The *Republic* is a long and involved dialogue. Plato was not prepared in the course of it to elaborate in detail his doctrine of pure pleasure in so far as such pleasure involved the senses. On the contrary, he wished to distinguish sense pleasure from philosophic pleasure. Odour was noted as an exception, since the sense pleasures in contrast to the philosophic pleasures are mainly impure (584 c). Had he instanced not odour but sight and sound, he would have been involved in further distinctions, i.e. exceptions to his exceptions, since the artistic pleasures evolved from sight and sound, as we have already seen, are according to Plato impure. Odour on the other hand does not furnish the basis of any artistic manipulation and could be cited without fear of ensuing complexity.

The potentiality of smell as a vehicle of beauty is moreover of some interest and calls for further comment. In the *Phaedrus*, sight alone is instanced as the sense through which we apprehend beauty. In the *Hippias Major* sight and hearing, to the exclusion of smell, are alone proposed. In the *Philebus*, smell, if less "sublime", is associated with sight and hearing as pure pleasure, and if pure pleasure implies, as it seems to imply, an apprehension of beauty, then smell in the *Philebus* ranks as a possible medium of beauty. So if the bodily senses be regarded as candidates for callistic dignity and the above dialogues as the electors, sight gains three votes, hearing two, and smell one. This order of merit accords very closely with our own feelings on the subject, and it should perhaps be observed that for the poet Keats not only smell but taste and touch were powerfully evocative senses; indeed, in this respect his poetry offers a striking contrast to Shelley's universe of light and sound. Plato, however, must certainly not be accused of inconsistency because he stresses the claims of different senses with varying emphasis. The underlying principle by which aesthetic potentiality is judged on each occasion is consistent. It relates to the clarity and distinctness of the impressions concerned. For only on the basis of clear and distinct impressions can the intellect operate. Sense must supply us with units, the basis of truth, and our pleasure in such truth is the elemental, objective apprehension of beauty. Sight pre-eminently possesses this basic clarity. At the same time, innate susceptibilities or subtle preferences acquired by experience may discover in the other senses sources of "knowledge" and satisfaction. What else are we to understand by a palate for wine or the connoisseur's discrimination in cheeses or blends of tea?

At this point our argument must enter upon a new phase. Plato's concept of intellectual beauty has been scrutinized with all the care that a work of these dimensions can reasonably devote to such scrutiny, and as a result we may affirm that, according to Plato, sense perceptions were in themselves beautiful just to the extent that they remained elemental and unelaborated, free from any associations with our appetites, predilections, and aspirations – that is to say in so far as they are dissociated from any aspect of our will. All intellection depends upon fundamental notions of kind and degree and the sense perceptions cited by Plato are such as supply us with these fundamental notions. Moreover, intellection is itself a pleasure quite independent of any function or moral purpose at which the will may direct it. By reducing our experience to its sense elements we so simplify it that similarities and differences of kind and degree are readily observed, and the detection of similarity in difference or difference in similarity is the basis of all intellection. It is in fact the sense of harmony which we were at the beginning of this chapter chiefly concerned to examine, an intellectual and at the same time aesthetic (callistic) principle. Bosanquet, as we have noticed, even patronizingly concedes that the sense of unity in variety is the one true aesthetic principle which Greek philosophy apprehended.

In Plato, this sense of harmony is the subject of a rather wordy analysis in Eryximachus' speech in the *Symposium*. Eryximachus supports his argument with a reference to early Ionian philosophic doctrine. The maintenance of physical harmony, he pleads, is the basis of medicine and agriculture. Music is founded on the same principle, as Heracleitus[1] seems to hint in his obscure pronouncement: "Unity is itself discrepant, yet reconciled to itself, like the harmony of bow and lyre." A discrepancy co-existing with harmony is a contradiction in terms. But perhaps, thinks Eryximachus, Heracleitus meant that originally discrepant high and low notes were brought into accord by musical art. For

[1] An early Bergsonian. Flourished in Ephesus about 500 B.C.

harmony is consonance, and consonance is accord; and accord and discrepancy cannot exist simultaneously. There may, however, be a discrepancy in which accord is potential. Such discrepancy affords a basis for harmony. In this way rhythm represents an accord formed from the discrepancy of fast and slow elements. The achievement of "love and concord" is in fact the work of music; and music may be considered as a science of love in so far as it is concerned with harmony and rhythm (*Symp.* 187).

The use of the word "love" to describe cosmic harmony is no impromptu whim. The terminology derives from Empedocles and is preserved for us in a fragment of his verse:

"All things converging at one moment in love, the next moment torn asunder in the hatred of strife." (*Fr.* 17. 7. D)

Thus Eryximachus lays both Heracleitus and Empedocles under contribution, and the relation of the Ionian and Sicilian schools which these two thinkers respectively represent can be precisely assessed by reference to a passage in Plato's *Sophist*, where we are given a more straightforward account than the whimsical mood of the *Symposium* permits:

"And so they (the early philosophers) tell us a fairy tale as though we were children. One of them claims that reality is a triad of which certain elements on occasion make some sort of war on each other. Love then supersedes and produces marriages, births, and the care of the young. But according to another theory, duality is the basis of existence, so that co-ordinates like wet and dry, hot and cold, are said to co-habit and breed. Our people of Elea derive their tradition from Xenophanes or even earlier; and their tales point to an actual unity that is multiple only in name. However, Ionian and, later still, Sicilian genius has deemed it safer to integrate the two principles and to proclaim reality as both one and multiple, a compound of hatred and love. The stricter spirits assert that states of discrepancy and reconciliation are concurrent, but others make a generous concession to our understanding by introducing an idea of alternation, according to which reality is at one moment united in love under the influence of Aphrodite, and at the next disrupted into multiplicity and strife." (*Soph.* 243 e)

Clearly Eryximachus tends to favour the Sicilian form of the theory, with its terminology of love and hatred, drawn from human relationships. Both Eryximachus and the "visiting lecturer" from Elea who leads the argument in the *Sophist* associate the ontological principle of unity in variety with Aphrodite. Eryximachus actually maintains that the influence of the two Aphrodites, "sacred" and "profane", as distinguished already in Pausanias' foregoing speech, extends into the realm of inanimate nature (*Symp.* 187 d). Now, as an eminent modern scholar[1] has remarked, Aphrodite "is more the goddess of beauty than the desire for it". Love (eros), as the *Symposium* makes quite clear, is the subjective need and passion for beauty as distinct from beauty in the object. What interests us here, however, is that both Plato and ancient Greek thought in general closely associated Beauty, in its objective as in its subjective aspect, with a sense of harmony which pervaded Nature, provided the basis of all art and skill, was requisite in all happy human and social relationships, and, as Socrates pointed out, was the sole principle by which man might hope to bridge the gap between the human and the divine. The concept of functional beauty as inspiring art and skill is particularly well illustrated in Agathon's speech:

"Love is a poet of infectious ability who inspires others to compose, and at his coming even those to whom no Muse has previously ministered burst into song. Does this not in substance prove him master of all musical creation? For he could not transmit to others what he himself did not possess or comprehend. Furthermore, his work extends to the whole of living creation, since who could deny that we owe

[1] C. M. Bowra, *Greek Lyric Poetry*. Oxford, 1936, ch. V, p. 189.

to him whatever is begotten or sown? The same applies to all craftsmanship; a brilliant future waits on Love's apprentices, but strangers to his touch will rest obscure. Love and desire taught Apollo his skill in archery, medicine, and prophecy; he too must be called Love's pupil. So also the Muses grew skilled by love of musical art, Hephaestus by love of the smith's trade, Athena by love of weaving, and Zeus by love of governing gods and men. Thus even the gods owe their accomplishments to the indwelling of love; and this love is the love of beauty; for ugliness is no concern of his. Before his time, as I said at the outset, those fearful deeds which legend ascribes to the gods, occurred under the sovereign rule of Necessity, but when this new divinity was born the love of beauty bred in gods and men all goodness." (*Symp.* 196–7 b)

In view of the passages which we have just quoted, there can surely be no room for a view which maintains that Plato's "erotic mysticism" bears no relation to his analysis of formal beauty in the *Philebus*. The sense of harmony underlies all beauty whether we understand it as accompanying a perception or inspiring an act of will. Yet it is all too easy to see in the formal, functional, moral, and mystical approaches to Beauty not different aspects of the same experience but different and even contradictory ways of accounting for it. Thus the Loeb editor[1] of Xenophon's *Memorabilia* writes in his preface:

"The doctrine of the Xenophontine Socrates is that all things Good and Beautiful must contribute to the advantage and enjoyment of man: nothing is Good but what is useful for the particular purpose for which it is intended. The very same doctrine is propounded by Socrates in the *Greater Hippias* (rightly or wrongly attributed to Plato), but on examination is rejected by him as untenable. But Plato in the *Gorgias* makes Socrates declare that a thing is Beautiful

[1] E. C. Marchant, *Memorabilia and Oeconomicus*. Loeb, p. xvii.

because it is pleasant or useful or both; and the doctrine is unchallenged. Lastly, there is a passage of similar import in the *First Alcibiades*. . . ."

Now, there is really no serious discrepancy between the attitude of the *Hippias* and the *Gorgias*. In the former dialogue the functional definition of Beauty is rejected, apparently on the strength of a sophistry, but really because, like other definitions in the same dialogue, it is not exhaustive. Later in the *Hippias*, Socrates proposes a definition of Beauty as pleasure apprehended by eye and ear – as we have seen. Clearly, the account of Beauty in the *Gorgias* is meant to embrace the two definitions which in the *Hippias* were offered as alternative. The factor common to usefulness and the pleasures such as are described is of course Goodness. Plato is relating Beauty to Goodness, though the limited space here devoted to the subject does not permit him at the same time to distinguish Beauty from Goodness as he does so carefully in the *Symposium*. Let us examine the pertinent passage in the *Gorgias*. The dialogue takes its name from Gorgias the sophist and rhetorician (Agathon's teacher), who had invented a prose style based on assonance and half-rhyme rather in the manner of G. M. Hopkins' poetry. An attempt to defend the practice of rhetoric as Gorgias understands it leads Polus, his young pupil, to champion an "amoralist" view of life which Socrates finds no difficulty in demolishing. Here is the portion of the debate with which we are concerned:

Socrates: Now what of this? All that is beautiful, whether in body, colour, form, sound, or activity, would, I take it, be classed as such by reference to some purpose. Bodily beauty depends in any particular instance on the power to discharge a specific service or to afford a pleasure in cases where the satisfaction felt by the beholder is a purely visual one. Does this account of bodily beauty seem to you exhaustive?

Polus: I have nothing to add.

Socrates: And so in all form and colour beauty is associated with the presence of pleasure, usefulness or both?

Polus: I agree.

Socrates: And a similar principle applies to sounds and musical effects, doesn't it?

Polus: Yes.

Socrates: And the same is also true of activities and laws. They are beautiful just in so far as they are useful, pleasant, or both.

Polus: I admit it.

Socrates. Perhaps also the same beauty is to be discovered in the pursuit of learning?

Polus: Of course. Your definition of beauty in terms of pleasure and goodness is quite correct.

Socrates. Ugliness then must be defined in opposite terms, those of pain and evil?

Polus: It must.

Socrates: So when one object exceeds another in beauty it does so by superiority in point of pleasure, usefulness or both?

Polus: Of course.

Socrates: Then it follows that when one object exceeds another in ugliness it does so through a preponderance of pain and evil?

Polus. Yes.

Socrates: Well then, consider what you said about sustaining and inflicting injustice. The former you proclaimed as worse and the latter as uglier.

Polus: I did. (474 d–475 c)

So Socrates has succeeded in establishing the principle of moral beauty. Polus' view that it is bad to be wronged but "ugly" to do wrong corresponds closely with the opinion accepted by Alcibiades in the first dialogue of that name (115 b, c) when he agrees that the desertion of a comrade in battle is a "good" but "ugly" act, while to succour him by an act of self-sacrifice is "beautiful" though "bad". This terminology is in contrast to our own, for unlike the Greeks we are conscious of strong moral implications in the word "good", while the moral content of the word "beauty" not only remains to be demonstrated but is often denied. It is no exaggeration to argue that for the Greeks beauty was primarily a moral term; and in support of such a statement we may cite their word for beauty's contrary, "aischos", which combines the meaning both of shame and ugliness. Beauty was for the Greeks pre-eminently the opposite of the shameful – a thoroughly moral conception.

Finally, it must be clear to anyone who has read the above passage in the *Gorgias* that the concept of formal beauty did not exist in Plato's mind as an alternative to moral or functional beauty. We shall perhaps understand Plato best, if we conceive of human experience with the aid of a mental diagram in the form of a three-edged pyramid. Each edge will represent one of the three cardinal values which Plato acknowledged – Truth, Beauty, and Goodness. These meet and become indistinguishable at the apex of the pyramid, that is to say, in the sublime (or "divine" as Plato has it literally). The human soul ascends to the sublime, as it were, spirally, beginning at the base angle of the edge of Truth, where formal beauty is to be discovered, and passes round by the way of the edge of Beauty – most clearly distinguishable in personal beauty – to Goodness, characterized by the delight in social law and order and morality in general. Man-made morality, however, falls short of the sublime and another turn of the spiral is necessary in order to reach the summit. The soaring spirit emerges once more on the edge of Truth, preoccupied this time not with simple harmonies of form but with the much subtler phenomena of philosophical and psychological adjustment. After this point the "beatific vision", described in the *Symposium*, supervenes, and the final step towards sublimity is conceived as a movement towards the Good,[1] the production of holy and truly philosophical life. However, at any point in the ascent all three values are in a sense present as long as the upward direction is maintained, for direction unites them. They meet at the same point, and this point can only be reached by a way which passes through all three of them. Beauty is thus stimulated by Truth and is itself a stimulus to Goodness. It is hard to understand aestheticians who deny the propriety of the term "moral beauty". Is there no difference between sanctity and mere righteousness? In the same way, the sense of formal beauty is separable from Truth. Plato saw beauty in geometry – but the average schoolboy feels differently. It is clear then that none of Plato's three cardinal values is adequate in itself, even though the emphasis of spiritual ambition falls now on one, now on the other.

[1] For the ultimate supremacy of the Good over Truth, see *Rep.* 509 a.

CHAPTER III

Plato's Evaluation of Art and Poetry

The connexion between this chapter and the last rests really in the fact that there is no connexion. That is to say, whereas we recognize a self-evident relationship between art and beauty, Plato recognized hardly any. Where he does in fact comment on art in point of beauty it is frequently to reproach works of art with their deficiency in this respect, as for instance in the following remark in the *Republic*:

"Neither by knowledge nor guesswork, then, can the imitator (i.e. the poet) discriminate between the beautiful and the vicious in relation to his own imitation." (602 a)

Such an attitude is possibly due to Plato's lack of sympathy with the art of his own day. In criticism of art he appeals to standards of formal beauty, which is apparently lacking in the work which he has in mind. In the *Laws* he austerely observes that pleasure and entertainment value are no substitute for truth and symmetry (667 e) and in the *Sophist* (235 d) he condemns what appear to be impressionistic practices in contemporary art. We shall not dwell on this aspect of Plato's criticism, partly because space does not permit and partly because the whole subject has been thoroughly treated in a book entitled *Platon et l'Art de son Temps*, by Pierre-Maxime Schuhl, professor at the Sorbonne. Suffice it to remark that a good critic, while not obliged to conceal his own tastes and predilections, should be able to distinguish these from canons of more general application. Plato was unable to do so and the quasi-metaphysical arguments which he advances in doctrinaire assertion of his own personal preferences will not bear scrutiny.

The obvious prejudice which Plato displays in his attitude towards art and poetry has in fact weakened his case against them and exposed him to the attacks and misinterpretations of modern critics whose prejudices run as strongly in the opposite direction. For instance, to blame Plato for accepting a view of art as "imitation" on the ground that art – according to modern assumptions – is essentially "creative" and not "representational" is at the best a mere anachronism. Art as "creation" is the reply of the atheistic liberal to the atheistic autocrat. It is the reply of Croce to Nietzsche. For both these thinkers in different ways found it necessary to replace humanized divinity with deified humanity, and in art Croce discovered man's claim to the divine faculty of creation. Such views, however, are only possible to atheistic systems, and Plato was not an atheist. Moreover, common sense is unquestionably on his side. Thus we read in the *Sophist* (264 c) that there are two orders of created things, human and divine. Reflection and shadow bear the same relation to material (divinely created) nature as artistic portrayal (imitation) does to practical crafts and their products. The neatness of the classification is to some extent marred by the recollection that the divine creations may also be objects of artistic portrayal, but the point of the observation need not be lost. Shadows, dreams, pictures, and other representations constitute an inferior grade of truth, in which the evidence of one sense cannot be confirmed by reference to that of another. In point of truth, then, art is inferior. The fact is obvious, so obvious that it was as preposterous for Plato to build an indictment of art upon it as it is for modern critics to deny its pertinence. We should be better enabled to assess Plato's solecisms at their right value if modern commentators instead of denying the essentially representational nature of art would recognize its phantasmagoric character as a drawback indissociable from specific advantages. That is to say, art sacrifices truth to aspiration and purpose. The intellect is drugged and placated

with a dream world in order that the will may exert itself with greater freedom than actuality permits. But to
Plato's objection that art is less "true", it may be answered
that from another point of view art is more true than actuality, in so far as it more truly expresses the will of the artist
and, perhaps, his public. On the other hand, the artist
presides absolutely over the universe of shadows which he
has evoked, and it is of consequence that he should be a just
ruler, exhibiting wisdom and integrity in his administra-
tion. This does not of course mean that every drama or
narrative should be a tale of "virtue rewarded", for it is
often preferable, especially in tragic art, that heroes and
heroines should die, saint-like, in credit with Heaven; it
means, however, that when Plato adopts a moralistic attitude towards art he cannot be lightly dismissed, as modern
critics would have us dismiss him, with a sweeping and
utterly untrue statement that art is concerned with beauty
only, not with morals.

It was observed in our introduction that, while Aristotle
was concerned mainly with "aesthetic" or the study of art,
Plato's strength lay in "callistic", his analysis of Beauty.
Consequently, we shall not expect to find in Plato the same
coherence and consistency when he deals with art and
poetry as we did when the various aspects of Beauty were
his theme. For our own purposes, however, we must adopt
some more or less orderly method in studying his treatment
of this subject, and we can hardly do better than begin with
a synopsis and commentary on the evaluation of poetry and
art which Plato offers us in the *Republic*. In this dialogue he
writes of artistic values at greater length than in any other.
He also writes with greater prejudice here than in any
other dialogue, so that what we have mildly termed an
evaluation of poetry and art might perhaps more aptly be
called an indictment of these faculties. The *Republic* has
always been controversial and it roused the antagonism and
indignation of art-lovers in antiquity as it rouses them today.

Its gross illogicality and unfairness are in themselves provocative. Its inconsistency with views expressed in other dialogues were noted by later Greek writers like Proclus. Modern scholars and critics appeal from it to the more indulgent attitude towards poetry which they think they discover in the *Ion*. Modern democrats – like the ancient democrats no doubt – are shocked by the Spartan and totalitarian criteria by which poetry is judged, and Plato's expulsion of poets from his ideal State is certainly answerable by an expulsion of "States" from an ideal world. Yet no champion of poetry has quite succeeded in disposing of the *Republic*. Most attempts to do so have themselves been based on misconceptions and false assumptions of the kind to which we have referred, but the pungency of Plato's indictment is due more than anything to the fact that Plato was himself among the greatest of literary artists. His dialogues are often dramas and his prose is often poetry. No matter how illogical or unjust the arguments of the *Republic* are shown to have been, the fact remains that a great writer of Plato's calibre could find it in his heart to despise writing. Moreover, his scorn was no whim of the moment. A large portion of the latter part of the *Phaedrus* is devoted to the deprecation of literary art. We must conclude that Plato counted his own literary genius as nothing beside the spoken word and personal example of Socrates. This is something which neither later antiquity, to whom literature was a substitute for political freedom, nor romantic modernity, to which literature is a substitute for religious faith, have ever been able to understand. Only, it is interesting to note that, in the *Republic*, Plato's denunciation of the arts is accompanied by a certain violence, suggestive of the celibate denouncing carnal lusts. To anyone who can write as Plato wrote, writing is a passion, and the cost of renouncing this passion was the measure of his bitterness. Not that he ever abstained from writing on principle, for the written word was conceded a certain mnemonic value; but he renounced the pleasure of writing as if it were a temptation, and the colder mathematical quality of later dialogues like the *Sophist*, the *Statesman*, and the *Theaetetus* is the evidence of triumph over what he must have regarded as literary escapism.

The theme of the *Republic* is Justice and the attempt to prove that a just man is inevitably and in every case happier than an unjust man. The dialogue is traditionally divided into ten books and the first book is occupied by a bitter and scathing argument with the sophist Thrasymachus, who, like Polus and Callicles in the *Gorgias*, puts forward the amoralist argument. Thrasymachus is defeated and humiliated by Socrates' powers of dialectic, but the question is immediately re-opened by Glaucon and Adeimantus (Plato's own brothers). They are in sympathy with Socrates' idealism, but require more substantial arguments from him, and for the rest of the dialogue they act as "devil's advocates" or sometimes mere point-by-point respondents as Socrates elaborates his case. In order to understand justice in the individual, it is claimed, one must first recognize the meaning of justice in the State; an attempt is therefore made to envisage an ideally just State and to outline the main body of laws and customs as they would exist in such a State. The State is deemed to consist of three social classes: the guardians or governing class, the military, and the menial. The three classes correspond to three elements of human psychology: reason, will-power, and appetite. The question of education at once arises, particularly the education of the governing class. Traditional Greek education was based mainly on the Homeric poems and Plato at once embarks on a systematic criticism of Homer. Many passages in the *Iliad* and *Odyssey*, he discovers, require censorship, especially those which represent the behaviour of gods and heroes unworthily. Plato also found that the various incarnations and metamorphoses of Greek mythology ran counter to his own concepts of changeless and impersonal deity. He would presumably have objected to Christianity on the same score. Modern commentators find it necessary to excuse Plato for basing his criticism of a poet on moral grounds, and it is pointed out that for the Greeks Homer and Hesiod were more than poets; they were sacred books, the main repositories for Greek religious tradition. This of course is true, and the fact that the poets were so regarded renders moral criticism especially pertinent. At the same time moral criteria in literary criticism do not need to be justified by any such special pleading, and the anxiety displayed by Plato's would-be apologists is often merely a measure of modern aesthetic prejudices. How easily we assume that beauty and morality are absolutely separable and that art is concerned exclusively with beauty! Yet we have already demonstrated by reference to Plato's own writing that the first of these assumptions is untrue. As for the second, it is alien not only to Plato but to classical Greek thought in general, and the Greeks may be allowed to have known something about art.

A more sweeping and general criticism made by Plato in this section of the *Republic* is concerned with different genres of poetry. Poetry put into the mouths of different characters, in the manner of drama or epic narrative, is condemned. If poetry is to have an educational value it must be didactic and the poet can only be an effective teacher when he speaks in his own person. This is a peculiar suggestion from a philosopher who chose dialogue as his normal method of instruction! However, Plato is here discussing junior education only, which, as he believes, is fundamentally religious. At a later stage in education it would presumably become necessary to foster logical ability rather than proclaim rigid principle, and for this purpose dialogue or even dramatic poetry, as he cautiously allows in the *Laws* (though not in the *Republic*,) had its advantages. A further philosophical stage in education is certainly envisaged in the *Republic*, and the transition from the indoctrination of the child to the cultivation of a manly critical independence

E

is an occasion of some delicacy and attended with difficulty (537 d). Plato's demand for poetic monologue seems to have been promoted by the notion that the good is unchanging and eternal and also by a rather strained application of the principle of "division of labour", already proclaimed as essential to communal efficiency. It would be damaging for a boy to recite poetry in any other character than that of "a good man", and as the business of the guardian class was to be good and wise, no useful purpose was to be discovered in training him for other ways of behaviour. This is one of the occasions when Plato's argument faintly suggests the illogical logic of *Alice in Wonderland*!

As a consequence of these decisions, however, Plato agrees to countenance dithyrambic poetry in his ideal State. The dithyramb was a kind of processional hymn sung in honour of Dionysus, and in the *Apology* dithyramb is condemned together with tragedy. Socrates here describes how, in a vain quest for truth, he approached first the politicians, then the poets, and finally the other craftsmen:

"After the politicians I approached the poets, writers of tragic, dithyrambic, and other poetry, and here I expected that my flagrant intellectual inferiority would be exposed. I used to cite those poems with which the writers seemed to have taken most trouble and ask them what they meant, in the hope of enlightenment. Gentlemen, I may not conceal the unhappy truth: the casual witnesses of our discussion were better able to expound those poems than the poets themselves. So I soon realized – to put it briefly – that their poetic ability was based not on wisdom but on some instinct or inspiration like that which we recognize in prophets or soothsayers, for in their eloquence they betrayed an incomprehension of their own words. Such, as it seemed to me, was the sad case of the poets. I also perceived that the successful poet considered his own intellectual supremacy to extend beyond the frontiers of poetry – which it did not – and I went away conscious again of the same measure of superiority as I had been aware of in my dealings with the politicians." (*Apol.* 21 e)

The superiority which Socrates claimed was of course the famous one – that he at least knew that he knew nothing. But the present interest of the foregoing speech lies in its condemnation of dithyramb together with other forms of poetry, although in the *Republic* (394 c) dithyramb is specifically commended as a genre in which the poet speaks in his own person. Such direct poetry does not fall under the general interdict. It would be wrong, however, to discover an inconsistency here. In the *Apology* Socrates is relating his own experience and the judgement which he passes on the dithyramb is pertinent only to the practice of contemporary poets. The criticism of the *Apology* is concerned with content only, not form, and the poets are blamed for what they taught or failed to teach, not for their method of teaching. As is evident in the *Laws* (701 a) Plato believed that dithyrambic poetry represented a healthy tradition which had been corrupted by its submission to the superficial criteria of a "theatocracy" – the mob verdict of the theatre which took nothing but entertainment value into account. The dithyramb, like other forms of ode and hymn, had at first preserved a generic form. But the uninhibited innovations of the poets had later led to a *confusion de genres* in which all liturgical or ethical sense had been lost. This poetry acknowledged no function and no standards save those of pleasure. Such apparently was the type of dithyramb which incurred Socrates' criticism in the *Apology*.

In the same way, an apparent inconsistency between the view of tragedy and comedy expressed in the third book of the *Republic* (395 a) and that which is attributed to Socrates at the end of the *Symposium* may be explained by a distinction between contemporary practice and ideal potentiality. In the *Republic* we are told that the same poet cannot be equally successful in tragedy and comedy, whereas the last incident recalled by Aristodemus in the *Symposium* is that of Socrates'

argument with Agathon and Aristophanes. The two playwrights, he recalled, were being driven to admit that the
tragic poet might in fact prove himself equally successful
in comedy. It would seem that in the Republic Plato has
in mind a circumstance which was true of the literary practice of his day, but that in the *Symposium* he was concerned
merely with potentiality. There was nothing – except literary habit – to prevent a poet from succeeding equally in
both tragedy and comedy. At the same time, Plato may be
fairly criticized – if one accepts the above view – for appealing to mere contemporary practice in legislating for a community which was itself an ideal potential. Such cruxes
occur in abundance in the course of Plato's discussion of
poetry and art in the *Republic*, and it is never quite possible
to judge how far he is and how far he is not consistent.

The criteria imposed on poetry in the early part of the
Republic are, towards the end of Book Three, extended to
cover both music on the one hand and the inert arts of
painting and sculpture – as well as handicrafts – on the
other. We know very little about Greek music, but it is
clear that the Greeks associated certain tonalities very
closely with certain human emotions and consequently
with these emotions as they were expressed in poetry.
Music, and frequently dance, nearly always accompanied
words, and our loss of Greek music is responsible for a good
deal of the difficulty which we find in analysing the metric
of Greek choral odes. This being so, we can easily understand Plato's criticism of poetry as being extended to embrace its musical equivalents. What is not so easy to follow
is its extension to the inert arts, for the strictures which
poetry has incurred in the course of the discussion have
been based very largely on its explicit and didactic aspects
– aspects which are much less apparent in painting and
sculpture and almost non-existent in the case of handicrafts.
Yet Plato felt strongly that the poetic and musical arts exerted the same kind of influence as the inert visual arts, and

a desire to clarify the relationship may be the reason for his unexpected return to the subject in Book Ten. Actually, Book Ten is anything but clarificatory. The reason is that Plato tries to say too much in too small a space. He never realized – as modern philosophers have realized – what a large subject "aesthetics" is. However, his association of the inert with the progressive or musical arts, obvious as it is to us, was not so to Plato's contemporaries. In Greek tradition, poetry and music together with history and education constituted the province of Apollo and the Muses; painting and sculpture were regarded as akin to handicrafts and needlework, and as such they came under the patronage of Athene, the practical goddess. In the tenth book of the *Republic*, Plato classes the two types of art together on the score that they are "representational". Modern instinct also classes the progressive and inert arts of entertainment together, but having a morbid horror of "representation", we explain their kinship more vaguely and less convincingly in terms of "expression" – for mere entertainment hardly distinguishes art from sport.

At the same time, it must be admitted that Plato in making his almost revolutionary classification enjoyed an etymological advantage. The ordinary Greek word meaning to "recite", "act", or "perform" a poetic or dramatic role (including danced representations) was "mimeisthai". Clearly, the word is germane to our "mime," though without any necessary implication of dumb show. Plato argues that the actor, speaker, or singer who "mimes" a part is in the same category as the painter or sculptor whose work "mimics" (again "mimeisthai") the works of Nature. The fact that the Greek word for recital or performance had the literal meaning of representation or imitation would seem to indicate that even before Plato the Greeks were aware of representation as a basis of kinship between the progressive and inert arts. The word "imitation", of course, in English, may imply commendation or the reverse. We speak of *The*

Imitation of Christ, but also of "imitation pearls". It has been argued that the Greek word, before it fell into Plato's hands, was always positive and commendatory and that it never had the meaning of deceit and imposture which it receives in the tenth book of the *Republic*.[1] Nevertheless, there is in all representation an implied notion of misrepresentation, inasmuch as representation falls short of identity.

Book Ten, then, opens with a reiteration of the dangers of "mimetic" or representational art, which Socrates claims have become clear now that the nature of political health and malady has been examined. He at once draws the parallel between dramatic and narrative poetry on the one hand and painted representations on the other. As we have observed, the word "mimeisthai" makes the transition very easy. A picture, it is claimed, is analogous to a mirror image, and the effort spent in producing something which can be produced so much more easily with the help of a mirror is wasted effort. The Theory of Ideas is invoked, and Socrates argues that three forms of any object present themselves to our consciousness: (1) the eternal and divine Idea of, say, a bed, the purely intellectual concept of a bed in its reality, (2) the object as it presents itself to sense experience, the bed of everyday actuality, and (3) the representation of the object as it is portrayed by an artist. A picture therefore stands at the third remove from reality. In the same way, Homer and the poets, even when their influence is not pernicious, are futile and useless. Their representations of human character and of human and social affairs stand in the same relation towards reality as do the painter's representation of material phenomena. It is also argued that poets and painters are concerned only with appearances. In order to know the reality of an object it is essential to understand its function as well. Thus there are three faculties connected with any object: the art of using it, the art of making it, and the art of portraying it. The first

[1] See H. Koller, *Die Mimesis in der Antike*. A. Francke, Berne, 1954.

two are concerned with the reality of the object as implied by its function, but the third faculty has no regard for function and use; it produces only an appearance and not the reality. Representational art is therefore an inferior faculty productive of inferior results.

Another consequence of the artist's foolish preoccupation with appearances is the irrational and emotional nature of art and poetry. Painting is full of optical illusion and the effects which it produces will not stand the test of measurement and mathematical assessment. We must not then be surprised if the representational arts, in renouncing reason, fall into the errors of mere emotionalism. A glance at the theatre is enough to confirm anyone in this opinion. The audience is accustomed to the enjoyment of unrestrained emotion in tragedy, just as it abandons itself to helpless laughter in comedy. This is the very reverse of what is desirable, for it has been shown in the earlier books of the dialogue that reason, not emotion, must be sovereign in the human soul; and by identifying themselves with the characters of tragedy and comedy as represented in the theatre the spectators ultimately come to resemble them, deteriorating into mere creatures of impulse and emotion, not of reason. Socrates concludes the discussion of art and poetry by reiterating the principle arrived at in Book Three, namely that dramatic or epic poetry can have no place in the ideal State. Only hymns to the gods and eulogies of good men are permitted; and that amounts more or less to didactic poetry. As if conscious that the case against poetry has been overstated – if not wrongly stated – he playfully suggests that the poets may be allowed to return if any lover of poetry successfully undertakes their defence either in a prose or verse composition of his own. Of painting and sculpture nothing more is said. The implication seems to be that they occupy the same position in relation to crafts and useful arts as dramatic poetry does to didactic poetry. The motive underlying this very unintelligent assessment of poetry and art lies in Plato's desire to discover a simple criterion for distinguishing good from bad art. The functional criterion at which he arrives is much too simple to be valid; and it leads him to contradict the much more plausible evaluations of "mimetic" art which he makes in other dialogues. For instance, in the *Republic* we are told that a poet is lower than a sophist and that a painter is inferior to a carpenter. Yet in the *Phaedrus*, as we have seen, in the passage where the various human faculties are assessed (248 d), poets and other representational artists rank higher than either artisans or sophists. Later in the *Phaedrus* also (268 d) the tragic poet is favourably compared with the writer of mere monologue. The essence of dramatic composition, we are told, consists not in writing mere speeches but in organizing diverse speeches into a unified and artistic whole. In the *Laws*, which, though it lacks the literary power of the *Republic*, offers us a far saner and more practical version of an ideal State, no automatic criterion of poetry and art is offered. Instead, tragedy and comedy are cautiously admitted, subject to reservation. Comedies will be acted because the citizens must see what kinds of conduct are ridiculous and to be avoided. The acting, however, must be done by slaves or paid foreigners, to ensure that the citizens themselves do not become conditioned by the ridiculous roles of the comic stage. He needs a long spoon who sups with the Devil! Tragedy, on the other hand, in so far as it portrays noble and dignified types of character, is in a sense competing with the social legislator and educationist. It is therefore firmly decreed that permission shall only be given for the performance of a tragedy after the application has passed before a censorship committee who will ascertain that the ideals and standards of conduct suggested by the tragedy are in accord with the ideals of the State itself. Each application is to be judged on its own merits (*Laws* 816 d–817 d).

It is unfortunate that the sections of the *Republic* in which

Plato deals with poetry and fine art represent his fullest and most systematic treatment of the subject, since a comparison with other dialogues makes it quite clear that they do not contain his considered opinion. Encouraged by this realization scholars have often attempted to save Plato's face by interpreting the *Republic* in terms more indulgent to the poet and artist. An example of such criticism appears in Professor C. Tate's articles in the *Classical Quarterly* (1928, 1932).

In these articles it is maintained that Plato in fact recognized two kinds of art – good and bad – and that these two kinds correspond to two kinds of "imitation" (mimesis), also good and bad respectively. The good imitation is the imitation of the divine Idea, the bad imitation is the imitation of mere sense phenomena. We read, apropos of the good imitation: "The guardians will be imitating their own ideal character, not characters utterly alien from their own. It involves not the suppression but the development of personality." Similarly, we are told that good poetry is imitative "because it imitates the ideal world which the philosopher strives to imitate and resemble in his own person. He (Plato) leaves it to be understood that the poet who imitates in the sense in which the guardians are permitted to be imitative will produce a direct copy of reality; he will be like the painter who uses the divine paradigm (cf. 500–1)."

Professor Tate's argument rests heavily on this "divine paradigm" which is referred to in two passages in the *Republic* (472 d and 500 e). The Greek word "paradeigma" meant exemplar or model. In Book Five, Socrates meets the objection that his "blueprint" for an ideal State cannot be translated into working terms. Just as a painting of a man may be idealized so that it corresponds to no model in actuality, so the plan for the ideal State may be formulated without reference to practicability. In the second passage it is declared that the true philosopher will regulate his conduct with reference to this ideal plan (paradeigma), regardless of the fact that no actual polity conforms to its standards. In the second passage particularly, the paradigm seems to be identical with the divine Idea, and as there is a clear allusion to the first passage it would seem that here the painter may be regarded as imitating the divine Idea of a man, just as the philosopher imitates the divine Idea of citizenship.

Plato, however, was hesitant about the application of his Theory of Ideas to sense phenomena, and Professor Tate's conclusions have by no means commanded universal assent. Shorey in his note on the first passage in the Loeb edition writes: "Plato is speaking here from the point of view of ordinary opinion, and it is uncritical to find here and in 501 an admission that the artist copies the idea, which is denied in Book Ten 597 e ff." This view is supported by references which show clearly that the Greeks commonly attributed the power of the artist to excel Nature not to his vision of an ideal but to his selective use of models, and the story is told both by Cicero and Pliny of how Zeuxis required five "sitters" in painting his famous picture of Helen. Such a procedure enabled a painter to associate the best face with the best figure, the best knees with the best ankles, even where Nature had not so associated them. One can hardly discover in this technique any mystical attitude corresponding to that of the unworldly philosopher, the citizen of the "City of God"; and Plato's analogy with painting is merely casual, not to be pressed too far.

On the whole, any attempt to credit Plato's discussion of art in the *Republic* with an intelligent basis leaves too much to be "explained away". Yet its very unintelligence is the outcome of Plato's awareness of certain issues which are often blinked by the modern aesthetician. If good art is indeed a power for good, then bad art is a power for evil, and to the extent that art is prevalent in any society it becomes imperative to distinguish between good and bad art, with a view to encouraging the good and discouraging the bad. In the *Symposium* (175 e) we hear that the Greek theatre accommodated an audience of more than 30,000 spectators and, although this is probably an exaggeration, it is clear that the Greek drama in Plato's day qualified for description as a "mass-medium". Plato was as concerned about theatrical performances as many reflecting persons are today about the influence of television programmes. No easy criterion of censorship, however, is to be discovered. One man's meat is another man's poison. The same work may contain elements which are inspiring and stimulating on the one hand, corrupting and degrading on the other; yet the two are often so intimately bound together that nothing can be excised. The view in democratic countries is that it is better to suffer the bad than to deprive ourselves of the good. Totalitarian countries, like ancient Sparta, have taken the opposite view, and one cannot say that one attitude is more logical than the other. Some kind of censorship seems inevitable, but the question in our day as in Plato's remains where and how to draw the line.

CHAPTER IV

The Poetic Process

From the *Republic* and the *Laws*, Plato's longest dialogues, it is natural to turn to the *Ion*, one of his shortest. An antithesis exists here not only in point of length but of content and treatment, for whereas the longer dialogues in their attempt to legislate for poetry are concerned only with an evaluation of the poetic faculty, the *Ion* briefly attempts an analysis of the poetic process without evaluating the process which it discovers. We may indeed find in Socrates' characteristic irony a certain measure of contempt, but on the other hand there are passages of lyrical rapture in which Socrates himself pays tribute to the sublime qualities of poetic inspiration; and these passages can hardly be understood as anything other than sincere. Another way in which the *Ion* contrasts sharply with Plato's attitude to poetry elsewhere lies in its association of the poetic with the beautiful. As we have already observed, such an association though natural to a modern aesthetician, is exceptional in Plato, who was accustomed to assess poetry in moral and rational terms. Modern scholars who are anxious to rescue Plato from charges of Philistinism turn with relief to the *Ion* to prove that the great philosopher's view of poetry was not really so different from our own. Plato, however, does not require rescuing; he was quite capable, in the *Laws*, of modifying the case which the *Republic* had mis-stated, and his normal "this-side-idolatry" attitude to poetry is not inconsistent with anything which is said in the *Ion*. At the same time, the *Ion* deals with another aspect of poetry. It is concerned, as we have just said, with the poetic process and with beauty in poetry, and in view of these facts it is reasonable to speculate that at least in Plato's opinion Beauty was to be associated with the poetic or artistic *process*, whereas its *function* could only be conceived in moral and rational terms. Such a view differs sharply from that of many modern aestheticians who profess to find in Beauty the be-all-and-end-all of art.

In studying the *Ion*, however, the modern reader will again feel that the subject is too big for the space allotted to it. Plato seems to realize the enormous importance of aesthetic problems without ever conceding to them the attention which their importance should command. Furthermore, in the minstrel, Ion, Socrates is provided with a fellow-dialectician as poorly qualified as the sophist Hippias. Admittedly, Ion does not share Hippias' intellectual pretensions, but he has unintellectual pretensions of his own, equally frustrating to any logical purpose. He is indeed a type one might meet among modern interpretative artists, pluming himself on his art but on very little else, both conscious of and content with his limitations. Moreover, Ion's illogicality seems infectious and Socrates is not always as fair or reasonable as he is in the *Hippias*.

Ion is an interpreter of Homer in two senses. Firstly he is a rhapsode – or reciter of poetry – and secondly he is an appreciative critic (530 c). He claims, however, that his skill relates only to Homer and not to other poets. Socrates uses this claim as a starting-point for his argument. He who can judge the merits of one poet correctly must be able to do the same for others, since judgement implies standards and criteria. This is true of all technical accomplishments, including painting, sculpture, the playing of musical instruments, and the art of the rhapsode himself (533 c). Socrates proceeds to analyse Ion's particular faculty. "Your appreciations of Homer", he says, "are not a matter of mere skill, as I previously suggested, but are dependent on some sublime power which prompts you. I would compare you with that stone which Euripides terms a Magnet – the

Heraclean stone as it is commonly called. As you know, it has power to attract iron rings. Moreover, it invests these same rings with a power similar to its own, so that they can attract other rings; and the result is often a long chain of rings suspended from each other, though in all of them the magnetic power is derived from the original stone. In precisely the same way human beings are inspired by the Muse, and from those who have been inspired a chain of similarly inspired persons is suspended. All the great epic poets uttered their poetry not in virtue of any skill, but by inspiration and divine possession, and the same is true of the great lyric writers. You may compare them with the sectaries of the Corybantes, who dance only when they are out of their senses. In just the same way the lyric poets are out of their senses when they compose their lovely songs. They embark on harmony and rhythm as on a Bacchic orgy, become possessed, and like the Bacchants, completely out of their senses, draw milk and honey from the rivers. Moreover, the poets themselves admit a spiritual process of this kind. They tell us that they cull their melodies from the mellifluous wells of the Muses' gardens and groves, and bear them to us, winged, like honey-bees. Indeed, they speak the truth. The poet is a light, winged, and holy creature, incapable of his task till the divine inspiration visits him and deprives him of his senses. For while a man is in full possession of his reasoning faculty he may neither compose nor prophesy; so that the compositions of the poet and the eloquence which he brings to his themes are no question of skill – as is instanced by your own appreciation of Homer – but represent a divine endowment. Thus each poet may succeed only in that kind of poetry to which the Muse impels him, whether it be dithyramb, encomium, hyporchema, epic, or iambic. In any kind but his own he will fail. Divine power it must be, and no skill; since were it a matter of skill, success in one kind would entail success in another. For precisely this reason the gods deprive such a man of his wits

before they make use of him, just as they do with holy
soothsayers and prophets. They want us to understand that
the source of their precious utterances is not the man himself, but the god who speaks to us through the man. This
was proved in the instance of Tynnichus of Chalchis, who
wrote no poem worth mentioning except the famous paean
which everybody sings, a work almost unrivalled in lyric
poetry. It was simply, as he himself says, 'an invention of
the Muses'. As I see it, the gods meant in this case to prove
to us beyond all argument that poetry is human neither in
its nature nor its origin, but divine in both, and that poets
are the mouthpieces of whatever gods may happen to have
possessed them. To demonstrate this truth, the god deliberately chose to put the loveliest of lyrics into the mouth of the
weakest of poets." (533 d ff.)

Ion readily agrees with this concept of the poet, and admits Socrates' further proposition that just as the poets are
the inspired interpreters of the gods, so the rhapsodes are
the inspired interpreters of the poets; and like the poet, the
rhapsode cannot be considered fully in his senses. Socrates
continues:

"Do you realize that the spectator is the final link in the
chain of magnetized rings? You, the rhapsodes and actors,
represent the middle link, and the first link is of course the
poet. Thus the deity sways men's souls as it will, and at-
taches them to each other by virtue of its power. As is reflected in the analogy of the Magnet, a rich concourse of
dancers, chorus-trainers, and assistant trainers attach themselves to that chain which is initially suspended from the
Muse. Indeed, different poets are attached to different
Muses, and we call this attachment 'possession' – which it
is. For the persons so 'possessed' are certainly 'gripped' by
the Muse. In the same way, the poets who constitute the
top links, Orpheus and Musaeus for example, support a
variety of inspired dependants, though the majority are
possessed and gripped by Homer. You, Ion, are of course

possessed by him, and when anybody renders the works of another poet, you go to sleep and can offer no comment. On the other hand, at the sound of Homer's music, you are immediately roused, your soul dances within you and your tongue is loosened. Your ability is neither a skill nor a science but a divine endowment, a possession. In the same way, the Corybantic sectaries recognize only the shrill melody of the particular god who possesses them, and at the impact of his song they become prodigal of gesture and utterance. The music of other gods means nothing to them. Similarly, you, Ion, are stirred only at the mention of Homer, and do not react to other poets. Your brilliant appreciations of this one poet are not the consequence of skill but of divine endowment." (535 e ff.)

This doctrine of inspiration is of course an elaboration of the comment in the *Phaedrus*, where Socrates, at the commencement of his praise of "love's madness" compares it to prophecy, religious frenzy, and poetic inspiration. Of the poet's power he remarks: "The third kind of possession and madness is that of the Muses. It lays hold on a refined and delicate soul and rouses it to a Bacchic transport which is expressed in odes and other forms of poetry, whereby the deeds of past generations are celebrated for the edification of their successors. But whoever knocks at the door of the Muses untouched by their madness, hoping that mere skill will make him a poet, will accomplish nothing. The poetry of the sane pales into insignificance before that of the mad." (*Phaedr.* 245 a)

In the *Phaedrus*, Socrates recognizes a sharp distinction between the type of madness which is an inspiration and divine favour on the one hand and the madness which is a pathological affliction on the other (265 a). In the *Ion* this distinction is not quite so clearly preserved, and Socrates ironically demands: "Can we regard a man as being entirely in his senses, when he stands up at a time of sacrifice or feast, draped with embroidery and crowned with gold, and weeps, though he has lost none of his gorgeous apparel and has nothing worse to fear than the presence of twenty thousand friendly persons none of whom is robbing or injuring him?" (535 d) In this colourful picture of the rhapsode in his glory there is an unmistakable note of contempt. Ion, however, is willing to admit the element of madness in poetic declamation; indeed it places him in some respects on a level with the poet he interprets. But he still steadfastly refuses to admit that his critical appreciations of Homer – that other aspect of his profession – are grounded in madness. Socrates now begins to argue with him in functional terms which recall the treatment of Homer in the *Republic*. The question is raised as to whether the rhapsode's powers extend to all Homer or only certain parts. Ion claims that all Homer is his province, and Socrates invites him to quote specific Homeric passages, which hold obvious technical implications, in so far as they relate respectively to chariot-driving, medicine, fishing, and soothsaying. Ion admits that he has no knowledge of these occupations and that therefore he would not be such a good judge of the accuracy of the passages in question as would a technical commentator. When pressed by Socrates to state what aspect of Homer his knowledge concerns, he professes to know such language as may suitably be attributed to man and woman, slave and freeman, ruler and subject (540 b). This is a reasonable answer. He might indeed have claimed a knowledge of professional types, as distinct from professions; but since he has been diverted from this, he takes refuge in social types. Socrates is not fair, for he insists on the professional and technical criterion, taking the example of a "man" who is also a ship's pilot, a "slave" who is also a cowherd (540 b, c). Eventually, Ion embraces with eagerness the idea ironically suggested by Socrates – that he possesses the knowledge proper to a military general. Clearly, such a notion is compatible with his own sense of dignity, but the *reductio ad absurdum* is not as absurd as it

F

might at first seem. Xenophon in his anecdotes of Socrates
reports the philosopher himself as arguing that a strong will
and an eye for character are the most important qualities in
a general, making, as they do, a good organizer, whether
for war or peace (*Memorabilia* 3.4). Ion also claims to have
an eye for character and to know what he likes within his
own sphere of activity, for example, his decided preference
for Homer. It is pertinent to observe that Xenophon's
Socrates actually specifies that a good chorus-trainer will
probably make a good general. Even if the same organizing
ability was not so important in a solo performer like a
rhapsode, Ion was at any rate called upon in the course of
his performances to dominate vast crowds. As we have
found occasion to remark earlier, an essential part of poetry
and fine art is concerned with the will of the poet or artist;
and this makes itself felt not as an action (as in generalship)
but as a communication. Ion's claim to military competence
may have been based on a sense that he also was required
to impress himself powerfully on his human environment.

In the second part of the *Ion* it is easy to see the characteristic Platonic approach to the subject of poetry – the functional utilitarian approach. The first part, however, in
which Plato develops his concept of inspiration, may well
seem so untypical as almost to constitute a heresy from the
point of view of normal Platonism. The difference, however, is one of approach rather than opinion. A modern
Dutch scholar[1] has drawn attention to an apparent discrepancy between the doctrine of the *Ion* and a statement
made by Plato in the *Laws* (719 c):

"Whenever a poet is seated on the Muses' tripod, he is
not in his senses, but resembles a fountain, which gives free
course to the upward rush of water; and since his art consists in imitation, he is compelled to contradict himself,
when he creates characters of contradictory moods and he
knows not which of these utterances is true."

[1] W. J. Verdenius, *Mimesis*. Leiden, 1949, p. 4.

The following commentary is offered: 'However, if it is the Muse herself who speaks through his mouth, it seems strange that the poet should involve himself in contradictions. There is no room for assuming a malignant intent on the part of the Muse, for Plato expressly assures us that "from every point of view the divine and the divinity are free from falsehood", and that "God is altogether simple and true in deed and word, and neither changes himself nor deceives others by visions or words or the sending of signs in waking or dreams" (*Rep.* 382 e). We can only conclude that the artist himself is to blame for confusing the inspiration of the Muse. This means that his state of being possessed is not absolute; the Muse does not completely direct his tongue and he does not completely lose his human character. Plato stressed the poet's dependence, but he certainly did not mean to represent him as no more than a speaking-tube in the mouth of the Muse. After all, he calls the poet her interpreter (*Io.* 534 e). Divine inspiration cannot reach the human world but through the poet's interpretation. Accordingly, a poem, though its origin lies beyond human control, does not mechanically reproduce a divine message, but it is the result of a contact in which divine as well as human activities are involved. Interpretation, the human aspect of the process of artistic creation, is easily attended by misunderstanding. The poet is a less able "maker" than his Muse (*Laws* 669 c). So if a work of art shows contradictions, this is an imperfection to be imputed to human weakness.'

This explanation, however, that the divine message is confused only by the human weakness of the poet who interprets it still does not account for the phenomenon of poetic inspiration as Plato saw it. If the weakness of the poet was responsible for the confusion, then the weaker the poet the more confused would be the message which he transmitted. But this is apparently not the case. For Plato has told us in the *Ion* (534 e) that the gods sometimes choose the weakest

of poets as a medium for the most lovely poems. He is therefore committed to the view that inspiration is independent
of human ability and may transcend human disability. The
contradiction between the notions of an all-wise beneficent
divinity and a divine inspiration productive of confusion
and deceit is not dispelled.

Surely a more satisfactory explanation of the apparent
contradiction can be obtained from the *Symposium* and the
Phaedrus. Plato tells us that god and man cannot really associate, and communications between them are carried on
by the agency of "daemons". Love is such a "daemon"
(*Symp.* 202 e) and it is logical to conclude that poetic inspiration, which in the *Phaedrus* is described as a "mania"
analogous to love, is another such. We should not then be
surprised that poetic inspiration – which is a lower inspiration than that of philosophic love (*Phaedr.* 249 d) – should
suffer from considerable confusion and distortion in the
course of its transmission through the realm of the daemons.
The theological propriety of regarding the Muse as a daemon need not greatly trouble us. If the fullness of her godhead was unimpeachable then, according to the doctrine of
the *Symposium*, her message would require a daemon to
carry it. However, if Plato had evolved his theory of daemons at the time when he wrote the *Ion*, its explicit development might have presented some difficulty, since the term
for poetic possession was "enthousiasmos" – possession by a
god – not "possession by a daemon". Etymology for once
was not on his side.

The very fact that in the *Ion* we find a theory of inspiration placed side by side with an appeal to functional standards should suggest that Plato did not feel his description
of the poetic process to be inconsistent with the application
of rational, moral, and utilitarian criteria. Not only in the
Ion but in the *Phaedrus* and the *Laws* it becomes quite clear
that Plato regards the poetic process as a form of hypnotism,
and this being so it was to some extent a blind force. Hyp-

notism itself is morally and rationally negative. It merely lulls our faculties, but in lowering the subject's own powers of resistance it lays him open to every kind of suggestion, and suggestions may of course be good or bad. In the *Republic*, Plato considers mainly the dangers of such hypnotism, and he speaks of poetry which is empty of content once the "musical colouring", the devices of metre, rhythm, and tonality, have been stripped from it (601 b). He terms such poetry "a kind of incantation", but later admits the delight of the incantation (607 d). Finally, if Poetry cannot be justified on any moral or rational basis, the hearer must keep himself alert and awake in her hypnotic presence by rehearsing in his mind the reasoned argument which demonstrates the danger of her power (608 a). On the other hand, we have already quoted from the *Phaedrus* to demonstrate that Plato regarded poetry as a divine and beneficial "mania". Here the hypnotic concept of poetic inspiration emerges with the utmost clarity, for in comparing it to the prophetic power of an oracle Plato refers to what was obviously a hypnotic phenomenon in ancient Greece. There can be little doubt that the Delphic priestess uttered her prophecies under the influence of an induced hypnotic trance.[1] The passage quoted from the *Ion* of course makes use of the same simile. Moreover, the Corybantic dancers also referred to in the *Ion* are another example of ancient hypnotic practice. The Corybantes were priests of the Asiatic goddess Cybele who worked themselves up into wild frenzies, in the manner of dervishes, through the use of certain forms of music and dance. In their frenzied state they were impervious to pain and practised barbarous acts of self-mortification and mutilation. Nevertheless, in the *Laws* (791) Plato tells us that those who followed their rites often obtained relief from morbid nervous afflictions, thanks to the hypnotic condition induced by their music and dancing.

[1] See R. W. Parke and D. E. W. Wormell, *The Delphic Oracle*. Blackwell, Oxford, 1956.

Humphrey House in his commentary on Aristotle's *Poetics* observes that "inspiration" is a word which "begs a great many questions". Plato felt much the same about it. The questions which it begs are all rational and moral – questions of directive – but there is no question of the power.

Was Plato right, then, in applying his matter-of-fact moral and rational criteria to poetry and art? Surely, we cannot seriously condemn Homer for lacking a knowledge of medicine or chariot-driving, or even for not being an infallible theologian! Yet the dilemma must be escaped somehow, and at least a partial answer to the question would seem to be given by Plato himself in the *Symposium*, where he names poetry as one of the products of sublimated love (209 d) and classes the poets Homer and Hesiod with the legislators Lycurgus and Solon as the parents of offspring "more beautiful and immortal" than the human kind. In the ascent to the sublime the successive steps taken by the philosopher-lover represent sometimes a progress in respect of Truth, sometimes of Goodness. Thus the lover who extends his passion from one particular favourite to personal beauty in general is advancing in Truth, for he is objectivizing a subjective urge, and the objective is the universal, the permanent, and the real. Poetry also represents an advance of this kind. Ion's exclusive devotion to Homer has all the caprice of a lover's passion, but by converting his audience to his own enthusiasm he bestows upon his personal feelings a wider reality. Truth is closely connected with communication. Subjective impressions, as Plato was well aware, represent an inferior degree of Truth, a half-truth which in the dialogues is often referred to as "doxa" or appearance. Truth is essentially communicable, and it is one of the first tasks of the lover – as is emphasized in the *Phaedrus* – to rouse an answering or requiting love in the object of his affections. The inspiration of love is thus communicated in different ways, sometimes to the personal object of love and sometimes to a third party. Poetic inspiration would seem to function in much the same manner, the achievement in either case being made in respect of Truth.

At the same time, the spiritual ascent described in the *Symposium* is also made in terms of Goodness – Goodness being conceived under the aspects of usefulness, morality, and sublimity. It is easy to see that legislation is "good", that it is moral or useful, and that in so far as the work of a great legislator like Solon or Lycurgus is an inspiration to succeeding generations it represents an advance towards the sublime. But what of poetry? What is poetry in terms of Goodness? Unless poetry can be demonstrated to possess some moral or useful content it must remain inferior to social achievements, for all the truth and objectivity which it confers upon personal caprice. This is the heart of Plato's dilemma, and it was the sense of this dilemma that caused him in the *Laws* to envisage the legislator and the administrator as rivals of the poet. The State also may be a work of art and an inspiration, and is of useful and moral consequence into the bargain. The force of such an argument can hardly be denied; without some moral or functional concept "inspiration" is indeed a question-begging term. If inspiration means anything it means a psychological compulsion which is in some way benevolent or beneficial. Without this "good" orientation compulsion is no longer an inspiration, and we should probably describe it more appropriately as "obsession". Remembering again that Plato classed both poetry and love as forms of divine mania, we may seek to explain his attitude to poetry in terms of his attitude towards love. In the *Phaedrus* we are made conscious of the dangers of love; the soul is drawn in two directions at the same time, and only the resolution of the true philosopher can maintain a steady upward progress in the direction of the sublime. It is clear from Plato's attempts to legislate for poetry, that he regarded this form of inspiration also as being beset by dangers and pitfalls.

Yet the fact remains that Plato classed poetry as a divine mania, together with philosophy, not as a merely morbid kind of madness; and this can only mean that he saw in it a potential inspiration, a source of Truth and Goodness. Indeed, it often seems that in the *Dialogues* Plato hits upon the answer to his own perennial problems without fully realizing that he has done so. Thus, if we ask whether the poet is in fact rendered redundant by the legislator, who creates in actuality what poetry only creates in dreams and shadows, the answer would seem to be found in the second and third books of the *Republic* where the educational possibilities are investigated. Despite much condemnation of existing poetry, it is stated that the right ideas can best be impressed on the minds of children through poetic fiction (377 a). It should have been only a short step from here to realizing that most men are children at heart and that for better or worse they were far more susceptible to inspiration through works of fiction and poetry than through Utopian political systems such as kindled the imagination of Plato himself. Admittedly, Plato had before him the example of Sparta, a city state whose laws and constitution survived throughout generations as an inspiration to all her citizens, tolerating no rival inspiration such as might have been fostered by any concession to the value of art or letters. The political single-heartedness of the Spartans was unprecedented and, even in this totalitarian age, perhaps still unparalleled. Yet Plato, though deeply impressed by Sparta, was very far indeed from an uncritical acceptance of the Lycurgan system. He could see what was good in Athenian freedom as well as what was bad, and in the *Laws* it is the Athenian citizen who leads the discussion, tactfully criticizes the prejudices of his Spartan and Cretan companions and is responsible for every constructive idea that the dialogue contains. Sparta in Plato's eyes was by no means a perfect polity, for all the power of the State to dominate the imaginations of its citizens. That is to say, the question of its inspiration is begged, just as the question of poetic inspira-ation is begged. Is the hypnotic force exerted on men's minds by a totalitarian government necessarily an inspira-tion? May it not be only an obsession? In the *Symposium* when Plato speaks of "activities and laws" as if they were occasions of inspiration (210 c) he is probably referring back to the poetry and legislation already mentioned as being the spiritual offspring of Homer and Hesiod and of Lycurgus and Solon respectively. As is clear from the *Ion* and other dialogues to which we have alluded, Plato real-ized that the hypnotic power exerted by poetry was far greater than that which political structures could com-mand. The political structure was easier to mould, control, and direct along moral and functional channels. Neverthe-less, while this thought dominates much of Plato's writing it is important to remember that he did not regard the poli-tical "work of art" as impeccable and that he did respect poetry as a potential influence for Goodness and Truth.

The relation existing between inspiration and hypnotic power is now quite clear. Moreover, it would seem that in-spiration is almost a synonym for Beauty. Beauty, like in-spiration, is a question-begging term. We distinguish it from Truth and Goodness, so that it is in essence irrational and amoral, divorced from all function. Yet it is only dis-tinguishable from ugliness in so far as it contains some ad-mixture of truth and goodness. The question is really a logical one. We may think of the beautiful as the opposite of the ugly or as superseding moral and rational values, in the same way that heat may be thought of as the contrary of cold or as a phenomenon distinct from light. No action or perception has any value except in so far as it is touched by inspiring beauty, so that Agathon in the *Symposium* speaks of all crafts and skills as being the product of a passion (eros). In the *Ion* we see that the poet and his artistic inter-preters differ from the exponents of other crafts and skills in so far as they do not convert their inspiration into rational, moral, and functional expression, but simply transmit it in amplified form. A poet in fact may be regarded as an amplifying (not a rectifying) valve for the voice of the inspiring "daemon". Yet some moral, rational, or functional quality must also be transmitted; otherwise inspiration is no longer inspiration but simply obsession. Such suggestions are none the less potent because they are subtle and defy analysis, and the danger that the public might be surreptitiously inoculated with obsessions and perversions masquerading as genuine inspiration was one to which Plato was very much alive. The danger is always present, yet the problem of how to combat it admits no simple solution. For who is the perfect critic? Plato saw clearly that the poet was not usually a good critic, and as Socrates remarks in the *Apology*, the man-in-the-street often shows a better understanding of a poem than the poet who produced it. Ion, the interpretative artist, fails not only as a critic of the moral and intellectual content of a work; he is not even a judge of its inspiration, for he goes to sleep when any poet save Homer is recited (532 c). The dynamic power of poetic inspiration springs from the poet's subjectivity, and this very subjectivity makes the poet a bad guide. In the history of literature poets have frequently been stimulating critics but rarely critics of balanced and catholic taste.

CHAPTER V

Aristotle on Art and Beauty

Any attempt to give an account of Greek callistic and aesthetic theory, as we have seen, necessarily involves systematization. Plato's views in any branch of philosophy whatsoever must be reduced to a system before we can readily study or understand them. He wrote in dialogue form and the problem of extracting his thought from its dramatic context does not differ very greatly from that of estimating the "philosophy" of, say, Euripides or Bernard Shaw. With Aristotle the case is different, for system and classification are the essence of his philosophic contribution. By ill luck, however, his *Poetics*, the work in which we might have expected to find an organized and exhaustive treatment of art and possibly beauty, has reached us in a mutilated and incomplete condition. Although the work itself is invaluable for the profundity of its suggestiveness and the acuteness of its distinctions, it remains a fragment to be eked out by whatever references to the subject can be gleaned from other Aristotelean treatises. Here also the commentator must be prepared to systematize. His task will admittedly be to recompose the pieces which originally formed a complete organism, whereas with Plato he must build with components which were never previously assembled. In systematizing, however, he is bound to interpret, and as an interpreter he may be resented. For the multiplicity of Aristotle's aesthetic interpreters and the confusion which they have bred has won interpretation in this domain a bad name. The student is inclined to feel with a Lutheran impatience that mediation merely stands between him and the light, and that Aristotle would be better understood if all forms of interpretation were swept away. Yet such a view, though deserving of sympathy, is inadmissible. The commentator on Greek Poetic Theory who does not try to reconstruct does nothing.

We should also at this point remind the reader of our general purpose, which is to recover from Plato and Aristotle a theory of Beauty and Art which may be offered as an alternative to modern aesthetic systems. Our objection to most modern systems is that they too readily equate the domains of Beauty and Art. This produces a dilemma. Either artistic beauty is superior to natural beauty or else it is a poor second best. The former alternative gives rise to capricious metaphysical systems and the latter leaves art without a *raison d'être*. The system which we have already derived from our study of the Platonic Dialogues does not fall into this trap. Art and poetry do not stand towards actuality in the same relation as Beauty does towards Truth and Goodness. The arts of representation are simply related to the three cardinal values in a different way. The effect of beauty in art is different from that of beauty in life, but artistic truth and artistic goodness also operate differently from the truth and goodness of actuality. For beauty is hypnotic, and the poet instils virtue and wisdom under hypnosis – a hypnosis which grips himself no less than his public. It so happens paradoxically that in order to assimilate the morality and wisdom of a poem our moral and rational faculties must be lulled. Hence Plato's distrust of poetry.

In turning from Plato to Aristotle we hope to discover not merely a confirmation but an extension and elaboration of Plato's system. There are many important aesthetic notions in the Platonic Dialogues, which for all their importance are touched upon very lightly, and in so far as we are able to discover the same notions elaborated in Aristotle we shall be nearer to establishing that Greek Theory of Beauty and Art which it is our avowed purpose to expound.

For instance, we have already observed the irrational quality of Beauty and artistic inspiration. But irrationality itself
is something that still needs to be investigated. Are we to
consider the irrational as the mystical and transcendent, or
as a pervading animal instinct, the expression of a primitive
élan vital? Or again, since we have associated the irrationality of Beauty with the irrationality of hypnotism, is it right
to consider the irrationality of art and poetry as something
physically and mechanically induced, as a hypnotic trance
is induced by a doctor or stage hypnotist? Another important question, still not thoroughly explored, concerns the
relation between the musical and poetic arts on the one
hand and the pictorial and plastic arts on the other. Let us
for convenience continue to call them, as we have done
already, the progressive and inert arts. As we saw, by closely
associating them as arts of representation, Plato in the *Republic* was revising the traditional Greek classification which
placed music and poetry in the realm of education but
painting and sculpture in the domain of handicrafts. However, when Plato wishes to stress the hypnotic character of
representational art he prefers to take his example from
poetry and music, where the hypnotic analogy seems more
apt. One is certainly conscious of an important difference in
method between the progressive and inert arts despite their
common representational basis, and this also is a question
in which Aristotle may be able to help us. Is poetry more
hypnotic than painting, and if so is it to that extent more
beautiful? But most important of all is the moral and
functional problem of poetry, which Plato raises without
ever precisely answering. If the *Laws* is to be regarded as
containing his last word on the subject, then he certainly
regarded tragedy and comedy as capable of moral edification. Yet his attitude is so cautious and suspicious, that one
cannot help feeling that he is no nearer here than in the *Republic* to defining what the moral and functional potentiality
of art really is. In the *Poetics* Aristotle dealt at length with

tragic drama, and his extant works also contain a number of important allusions to comedy and the nature of the ridiculous. It is here, if anywhere, that we shall find an assessment of poetry in moral and functional terms, for, as Plato pointed out, it is above all in dramatic poetry – as distinct from merely didactic poetry – that the moral and functional standards of actuality cannot apply. Let us take the opportunity of stressing once more our main thesis: art and poetry are essentially moral and functional, but not in the same way as other skills. Aristotle will help us far more than Plato to understand the nature of this subtle difference.

At the same time it is desirable to show in what sense Aristotle confirms Plato's view of aesthetic and callistic values. It is all the more desirable since Aristotle is often regarded as correcting or contradicting Plato on this subject. Indeed, it is true to say that a great deal of Aristotelean philosophy consists in modifications and amendments of Platonic concepts, and Aristotle himself is certainly at no pains to conceal his differences from Plato. In the *Poetics* there is no mistaking the polemic tone with which he assumes the defence of representational art. Yet here he can hardly be blamed, for had not Plato himself issued the challenge, when in the *Republic* he invited an apology for poetry from those who were "not poets themselves but lovers of poetry"? The challenge that was made in a debating spirit could only be met in the same mood. Moreover, this should remind us of a fact which we have already demonstrated: the *Republic* does not represent Plato's *considered view* of poetry, and although Aristotle's *Poetics* in some respects contains an answer and refutation of the notions formulated in the *Republic*, it does not run counter to those doctrines of beauty and inspiration and moral value in art which we have identified as fundamental in Plato's attitude.

One of the most obvious occasions on which Aristotle subscribes to the Platonic theory of Beauty is to be found in the

Nicomachean Ethics (117 b 16), where Aristotle in dealing with the philosophy of pleasure endorses the distinction made in the *Philebus* between "mixed pleasures" which imply some degree of agonized anticipation and the pure pleasures of sight, hearing, and smell. Aristotle writes: "It seems that pleasure is implied in the relief of some initially distressing privation. Yet this is not true of all pleasures. For no pain is associated with the pleasures of learning, smell, hearing, and sight. . . ." Plato, it will be remembered, also included in the unmixed pleasures our delight in learning and in geometrical regularity of form. It is interesting to note that Aristotle elsewhere associates mathematics with the sense of beauty; for in the *Metaphysics* (1078 a, b) we read: "Goodness and beauty are different, the former being present in action, the latter in things that are motionless. Thus those who claim[1] that the mathematical sciences are not concerned with goodness and beauty miss the truth. For mathematics pronounces and demonstrates on such matters in a marked degree. True, it may not deal with the concrete embodiments, but it is by no means silent on underlying principles. For instance, the greatest species of beauty are order, proportion, and limit, which are above all the objects of mathematical research." Aristotle goes on to argue that, since order, proportion, and limit are fundamental "causes" of existence, beauty is in the same way to be treated as a fundamental cause. The passage is of special interest when read in conjunction with the well-known statement in the *Poetics* (1450 b 37) that beauty is to be found in size and order. In the *Topics* (116 b 21) Aristotle proclaims proportion (symmetria)[2] as the basis of melody; or perhaps he is speaking of proportion in the disposition of the limbs. It depends how one translates "mele". The general tenor of all such remarks, however, is to confirm the doctrines which we have deduced from the *Philebus*

---

[1] The Cyrenaic philosophers. See *Metaphysics*, 996 a 32.
[2] Cf. *Politics*, 1302 b 33 and *Problems*, 916 a.

and the *Hippias Major*. There is a primitive harmony to be discovered in certain objects of the phenomenal universe, of which beauty is an aspect or ingredient.

When we come to study beauty in its relation to art, we still find in Aristotle Platonic and Socratic echoes. In the *Politics* (1281 b 10) one reads: "Men of high character excel the majority in the same way that those who are handsome are reputed to excel those who are not, and in the same way that the creations of the artist excel the living model. The secret lies in the assembly and unification of features otherwise dispersed; for taken separately the eye or any other part represented by the painter may compare unfavourably." The idea of symmetry and propriety in art is again stressed apropos of political equilibrium in *Politics* 1284 b 8: "A painter would not concede to his subject a foot which was out of all proportion even if it was an exceedingly beautiful foot; and a shipbuilder would exercise the same restraint as regards the stern or any other part of the vessel he was constructing. In the same way the conductor of a chorus would not welcome any member of it who could sing better and louder than all the rest put together."

These remarks are interesting for their insistence on proportion. In the interview between Socrates and Parrhasius, as described in Xenophon's *Memorabilia*, it is agreed that the painter selects the most beautiful details from several models and combines them. Aristotle slightly amends this view of the artistic method. Although he agrees that the artist may select from a variety of models, the selection made is not one of the "most beautiful details" but of those which will combine to form the most beautiful whole. Nevertheless, our purpose here is to demonstrate similarities between Aristotelean and Socratic or Platonic views rather than to distinguish them, and we made the allusion with this object in mind. The two passages show clearly that for Aristotle beauty was a legitimate consideration in art, as it was for Plato (*Rep.* 472 d). Of course, those of us who are dominated by modern assumptions will find that this is to credit him with no more than a platitude; but it is something which should be borne in mind when we are tempted to identify Aristotle with an exclusively "imitative" concept of art where truth and not beauty is the ultimate criterion, or when Greek aesthetic concepts are held to have been vitiated by exclusively ethical judgements. Far from that, the Greek view, as it emerges in the writings of Plato and Aristotle, was extremely well balanced, and one-sidedness is to be discovered in the modern critics' obsession with purely callistic standards.

Functional concepts of beauty, which, as we have seen, represent another aspect of formal beauty, abound in Aristotle. Not only is function the principle of artistic beauty but of personal beauty also. "Standards of beauty", he tells us, "vary according to a person's age. In the young, beauty implies the possession of a body apt for exertion, whether of speed or power, while the possessor himself affords pleasure to the eye. That is why all-round athletes are the most beautiful – because they are built for power and speed. A man in his prime, however, should be formed for warlike exertions, and his appearance should be at the same time pleasant and formidable; while an old man should be equal to such exertions as are unavoidable, and inoffensive in so far as he is free from the common disfigurements of old age." (*Rhet.* 1361 b 8)

A man's appearance must thus express qualities appropriate to his age, if he is to conform to Aristotle's canon of beauty. The unifying principle in proportion is to be discovered in the function to which the whole organism is directed. Not only a particular age in life but also a social status carries with it a notion of function. In the *Politics* (1254 b 28) Aristotle declares that the purpose of Nature is to make the bodies of slaves different from those of free men. The slave's body is powerfully built for the performance of essential labour; the typical free man on the other hand is

G

erect and not physically adapted to such services; his body is suitable for a life of citizenship, that is, for serving the State in peace and war. Aristotle goes on to observe – perhaps with the wistfulness of the theorist who realizes the limitations of theory – that in practice the slave often possesses the free man's body and vice-versa. If free men were as physically distinct from slaves as were the statues of the gods from human beings, then there would be no difficulty in assigning servile and citizen duties where they belonged. Unfortunately, he concludes, beauty of soul is not so easy to detect as beauty of body.

Beauty of soul of course implies the notion of moral beauty, that point at which standards of Beauty and Goodness seem to merge. Aristotle, like Plato, is conscious of this point at which the two fundamental values become indistinguishable. In the *Nicomachean Ethics* we read (1099 a 12): "Everybody takes pleasure in the thing which he loves. The horse-lover takes pleasure in horses, the lover of spectacle in spectacle. In the same way the lover of justice takes pleasure in justice and the lover of virtue in virtue generally. In most persons, however, pleasures are at war because they are not pleasurable by nature, while those who love beauty take pleasure in natural pleasure. Such pleasure is found in acts of virtue, which afford pleasure by their very nature to those who can enjoy it. The life of these persons does not require pleasure as an appendage, for it contains pleasure within itself. Moreover, anyone who does not take pleasure in beautiful actions is not good. . . ." There is certainly a Platonic ring in these lines. The ultimate identity of beauty and virtue which Aristotle here proclaims recalls the doctrine of the *Symposium* – and indeed many other Platonic ethical pronouncements. It is true that Aristotle hesitates as to how far "external goods" are necessary to complete happiness, whereas Plato was always eager to disown such dependence on externals. The view expressed in the *Nicomachean Ethics*, however, is that goodness and beauty lie within the reach of the normal man and can be attained by the art of virtue. Indeed, identification of beauty and virtue is far from infrequent in Aristotle. Young people are described in the *Rhetoric* (1389 a 12) as preferring beautiful to profitable actions, for "calculation aims at profit, virtue at beauty". In the *Nicomachean Ethics* again (1143 a 16) he observes quite casually, as if as a matter of course, that what is well done is "beautifully" done.

It should be clear from the foregoing considerations that Aristotle recognized Beauty as a prime value in life and art. At the same time Beauty never quite attains the independence in Aristotle's philosophy that it does in Plato's. For Aristotle, Beauty is always linked with the rational and the moral. There is nothing in his writing which corresponds with Plato's association of Beauty with love, and through love with "mania". On the other hand, the irrational impulse towards reason and knowledge themselves receives even greater emphasis from Aristotle than it does from Plato. As we saw in the *Philebus*, Beauty was specified as the pleasure felt in simple perceptions and inferences. Aristotle has much to tell us of the instinctive delight which the mind takes in reasoned processes, though he never actually identifies such delight with the sense of beauty. The question, however, is perhaps simply one of terminology, for when beauty is associated with rationality and rationality itself is the outcome of an inexplicable impulse and the satisfaction of an unreasoned desire, then we can hardly fail to equate the sense of beauty with this obscure impulse.

In this connexion the most significant passage is to be found at the beginning of the *Metaphysics* (980 a 1). All men, says Aristotle, naturally desire knowledge. Evidence for the fact lies in the satisfaction which we take in sense perceptions. Sense perceptions are valued for their own sake apart from any ulterior advantage which they may afford, and this is especially true of the faculty of sight. More than any other sense, sight fosters knowledge and presents us with distinctions. We of course share sense perceptions with the animals, and this in some animals is supplemented by memory, though others do not possess memory. Animals which possess the faculty of memory are more amenable to reason and are more susceptible to training than those which do not. Some animals exhibit rational characteristics, although they cannot be taught. This class includes bees and all such as are unable to distinguish sounds, for teaching is addressed to the memory and depends upon the sense of hearing. Those creatures which cannot be taught live by their power to visualize and memorize but scarcely partake of anything that can be called "experience". The human race, on the other hand, lives by art and calculation, and memory is the source of experience or empirical knowledge in human beings; for an accumulation of memories constitutes empirical knowledge. Thus it would seem that empirical knowledge approximates to art and science. But it would be more accurate to say that men arrive at art and science through empirical knowledge. Art comes into being when, as a result of many empirical apprehensions, a universal judgement is applied to instances classifiable in virtue of their similarity.

In relation to this passage the reader should perhaps be warned of certain difficulties of translation. Aristotle's classification of faculties does not correspond to our own. Empirical knowledge (empeiria), art (techne), and science (episteme) represent an ascending scale of rationality. Art, so understood, has little to do with our concept of Fine Art and might be better translated simply "skill" or "technique". It included such faculties as navigation and medical ministration. Aristotle's distinctions are in fact clear and useful and their adoption today might save us from a great deal of nebulous thinking – for instance from trying to erect a science of education when teaching obviously lies between "empeiria" and "techne", or from issuing diplomas in "hôtellerie" or poultry-keeping. However, we have referred to the passage with a view to demonstrating Aristotle's concept of rationality as an impulse. The roots of this impulse are even sub-human and are to be discovered in the animal world itself. It is made clear, however, that the higher forms of intelligence are more general, more teachable, more abstruse, and less useful than the lower. For wisdom, the goal of the philosopher, is an end in itself and serves no other science or faculty.

"It is clear," says Aristotle (982 a 10), "from a consideration of those who first pursued wisdom, that it is not a creative faculty. Originally, as now, men were stimulated to philosophy by a sense of wonder. The everyday incongruities of life first roused this sense, and thinkers were led on by degrees to study wider subjects, such as the phenomena affecting the moon, sun, and stars and the origin of the universe. Bewilderment and wonder beget a consciousness of one's own ignorance, and it follows that the philosopher is also a lover of myth; for myth is compact of wonders. Now, since the object of philosophy is an escape from ignorance, it is evident that men pursued knowledge for its own sake and not for any incidental utility. The facts prove it. This particular type of intelligence was esteemed only when the demands of utility on the one hand and leisure and amusement on the other had already been satisfied. Obviously, then, the pursuit of wisdom has no ulterior motives; it exists in the manner of a free man, who lives at his own behest and nobody else's; and in this way, alone of all the sciences it is to be considered free, since it alone exists for its own sake. The possession of it might therefore be regarded as something beyond human power, for in many ways human nature is in bondage. Thus Simonides says: 'This prize belongs to god alone' and man has no right to expect the assignment of knowledge to himself. Indeed, if the poets are right and divinity is jealous, we might assume that those whose knowledge was excessive would be unfortunate. But divinity cannot be jealous. On the contrary, as the proverb runs, poets often speak false; neither is any faculty more estimable than that of which we are speaking; for it is divine and estimable above all others."

Aristotle stresses the divine nature of philosophy. Since godhead lies presumably at the origin of the created universe and is concerned with its prime causes, it is reasonable to assume that any knowledge possessed by God would be concerned with such origins and causes; and consequently philosophy, which is the study of prime origins and causes, has every right to be considered divine. A nice distinction is here drawn between the good and the useful; for Aristotle maintains that while philosophy is the least useful of sciences, it is at the same time the best (983 a 10). The irrational nature of the divine (theion) thus becomes evident. Philosophy, or at any rate wisdom, which is its object, is good for no reason, but simply by virtue of its inherent goodness. Thus our rational faculties are not only promoted by an irrational instinct but are directed towards an irrational goal. The exercise of reason is itself an inexplicable compulsion bounded at one extreme by primitive impulses and at the other by philosophic exaltation.

Now, according to Aristotle, the arts of leisure and entertainment represent a more philosophic and therefore more elevated faculty that do the useful arts. He tells us that the pioneers of art excited wonder not by the usefulness of their discoveries but simply because they were outstandingly wise (981 b 13). This is another way of saying that such arts excite wonder. The element of wonder and the circumstance of "uselessness" are both philosophic characteristics. Aristotle's remarks on the subject of wonder are of great interest, and when Aristotle speaks of wonder as being the impulse towards knowledge it would seem that he meant by the word something very similar to what Plato meant when he spoke in the *Symposium* of a "love" or passion for know-

ledge. Wonder is pleasant (*Poet.* 1460 a 17). Wonder is the
basis of myth (*Met.* 982 b 19). In epic poetry wonder has a
special place because epic most easily accommodates the
irrational element (*Poet.* 1460 a 13). In the *Metaphysics* an
occasion for wonder is discovered in the fact that the diagonal of a square is not equal to its side, or that in mathematics there can be no measurement of a minimum unit.
Such phenomena of course excite wonder only in the uninstructed, for Aristotle hastens to point out that the mathematician would feel considerable wonder should the facts at
any time appear to be reversed (983 a 20).

An example of wonder provoked by irrational incidents
in epic poetry is afforded by the flight of Hector from
Achilles while the entire Greek army, at a gesture from the
latter, accept the role of motionless spectators (*Iliad* 22. 205).
Our feelings about such incidents are mixed; for though the
wonderful is pleasant, wonder only fosters the rational by
flouting it, and there is a limit to the amount of wonder that
our rational instincts will tolerate. Thus the scene mentioned is tolerable in narrative but would not be so on the
stage (*Poet.* 1460 a 14). In order to appreciate Aristotle's
point we have only to compare a reading of the final act in
Hamlet with a producer's attempt to cope with petrified
courtiers and soldiers in the closing scene. As a further instance of epic irrationality Aristotle alludes to the episode
in the *Odyssey* where the sleeping Odysseus is deposited without his knowledge by well-intentioned Phaeacians on the
shore of Ithaca (*Od.* 13. 116). The improbability here is so
formidable that only Homer's brilliant handling of the incident makes it acceptable (*Poet.* 1460 b 2). It would appear
that, in the face of bleak incongruity, nothing but the poet's
skill can save the situation.

Incongruity, something out of place (atopon), appears to
be the essential occasion of wonder. Our experience presents us with an incongruity and forces an appeal to reason.
Rule of thumb (empeiria) might suggest that the diagonal

is equal to the side, but measurement proves otherwise. Reason must supply an explanatory principle. In myth and the poetry which enshrines it, traditions representing the mystery and obscurity of human origins in terms of irrational incident are felt to be incongruous with our direct experience of life. Thus our awareness of reason and our pleasure in it are first stimulated by a heightened sense of the irrational. He who wonders is conscious of his own ignorance and philosophizes to escape from it. In the same way, perhaps, a sense of immorality is the normal approach to morality; and we may compare the love of beauty, which is first felt as a privation. Clearly, the sense of wonder fostered by poetry explains the philosophic quality which Aristotle attributes to poetry. His well-known dictum that poetry is a more "philosophic faculty than history" (*Poet.* 1451 b 5) confirms this attitude and we have seen that the philosopher (literally "the lover of wisdom") – like the lover of poetry – is also a lover of myth. The poet, however, is not a philosopher, and in the *Poetics* we are told (1448 b 14, 15) that although the pleasure afforded by poetic representation is a rational pleasure, the ordinary man – for whom presumably poetry is destined – is capable of such pleasure only in a reduced degree. It would seem that the main object of poetry is to excite wonder rather than to satisfy it, and this is interesting, for wonder amounts to fascination and in such fascination we discover a hypnotic quality closely allied to the poetic "enthusiasm" which Plato describes in the *Ion* and to which Aristotle himself – as we shall see – elsewhere alludes. At the same time there is an important difference between this process of stimulating the reason without fully satisfying it and the process of suppressing reason in order to reduce the resistance of our rational habits to new rational suggestions. In one instance the hypnotic power seems to be initially generated by exciting the reason, in the other by lulling it. There is evidence that Aristotle recognized both these processes, for he refers to another irrational element in poetry, apart from that of "wonder". In fact, like Plato, he speaks of "divine possession" (entheon, enthousiasmos). Let us examine some of these allusions.

One of the relevant passages (in the *Poetics*) is already very well known and has been the subject of much comment, partly perhaps because it contains a celebrated textual emendation. We wish, however, to plead for a translation which differs from the English rendering normally advanced and to understand by the word "or" the meaning "or even" – not "or else." Reading in this way we have:

"It follows that poetry is the product of a mind naturally endowed *or even* abnormally constituted. Persons naturally endowed are highly impressionable and abnormal types are liable to wild emotional transports" (literally, "are ecstatic"). (*Poet.* 1455 a 32)

The meaning becomes clearer if we place beside it another of Aristotle's psychological observations taken from the *Rhetoric*: "Naturally endowed families degenerate into abnormal types, as appears in the descendants of Alcibiades and Dionysius the First; while stable generations are succeeded by stupid and inert descendants, as is instanced by those of Cimon, Pericles, and Socrates." (*Rhet.* 1390 b 30)

Here also natural brilliance is associated with abnormality or "mania"; and the brilliant and abnormal characters are not contrasted with each other so much as with the stable and inert characters. S. H. Butcher says that Aristotle in the above passage in the *Poetics* distinguished between "two classes of poets – the man of flexible genius who can take the impress of each character in turn, and the man of fine frenzy, who is lifted out of his proper self, and loses his own personality". Do two such classes of poets really exist? It is certainly hard to discover two such types in ancient Greek poetry, unless one regards the lyric poets as "ecstatic" and the dramatic poets as impressionable or "euplastic"!

But Aristotle is here discussing the dramatic poets and there is not the least evidence for any such application of his remarks. Surely, the truth is that he mentions two *degrees* in the same class. It is customary with him to describe a psychological type in terms of (*a*) its normal characteristics and (*b*) its extreme or abnormal manifestations. This one psychological type, impressionable at the best, neurotic at the worst, constitutes a volatile class which is distinguished by implication from the other, stable class of personality referred to in the *Rhetoric*. If we accept this view we are confronted by a notion of poetic temperament very similar to that which emerges in Plato's *Ion*. The poet is irrational, and suggestible because he is irrational. Similarly we are told elsewhere that a certain poet, Maracos of Syracuse, was more successful when transported out of himself (*Probl.* 30 1, 954 a). The verb used is again cognate to our word "ecstasy". Furthermore, there are occasions when Aristotle describes poetic power in Plato's terms of "divine possession" (entheon, enthousiasmos). He tells us in the *Rhetoric* that the orator makes use of poetic diction since it exercises a fascinating ("enthusiastic") effect upon his audience. The orator has this much in common with the poet, for poetry is a question of "divine inspiration". It is "entheon" (*Rhet.* 1408 b 19). Towards the end of the *Politics*, also, Aristotle speaks of "enthusiasm" in connexion with musical tonality (1341 b 33). It should be noticed, however, that the hypnotic notions of "ecstasy" and "enthusiasm" occur only in connexion with the progressive arts – poetry, music, and dancing. Are we then to infer that these arts avail themselves of the hypnotic method in which the mind is rendered suggestible by a degree of initial stupefaction, while the inert arts of portrayal, like painting and sculpture, fascinate us by stimulation of the rational faculties? If so, poetry – and especially dramatic or narrative poetry – would seem to occupy a midway position between the progressive and inert techniques, and in pursuing this distinction we can hardly do better than turn to Aristotle's *Poetics*, where dramatic and narrative poetry receive special attention, and where there are plentiful comparisons with music on the one hand and with painting on the other.

CHAPTER VI

Mimesis and Rhythm

It seems preferable in studying Aristotle's *Poetics* to avoid the word "imitation" and use a transliteration rather than a translation of the Greek word, thus – mimesis. "Imitation" is a good translation, for it conveys wide varieties of meaning as does the Greek word. It does not, however, convey the Greek meaning of musical or poetic recital without any clear reference to the representational aspect of such recital, and on the other hand it does not imply lack of originality, as does our word "imitation" when used in connexion with art or poetry.

Aristotle remarks early in the *Poetics* that poetry springs from two natural causes (1448 b 5). The text, as often in the *Poetics*, is elliptic and obscure. We can only start by offering a translation: "Poetry seems to have sprung from two causes, each of them rooted in Nature. Mimicry (mimeisthai) is natural to human beings from childhood upward, and man surpasses all other animals precisely in respect of this faculty of mimicry. Through the mimetic faculty he learns his first lessons, and everybody takes pleasure in mimetic representations. So much is clear from our experience. For subjects unpleasant in themselves (e.g. uncouth animals and corpses) are pleasant to contemplate in pictures, precisely when portrayed in greatest detail. The reason is that the philosopher's enjoyment of learning extends itself to the common man; who, however, partakes of it in shorter measure. He is entertained by pictures because in contemplating them he learns and draws conclusions as to the identity of an object. He identifies for instance the figure in the portrait with that of the sitter. If he has not seen the sitter, then he does not value the picture as a portrait, but in virtue of its finish and colouring or some other property which it possesses. It is natural for us to take pleasure in mimetic representation as well as in harmony and rhythm; for metres are clearly species of rhythms. Poetry thus originated with a gradual advance on impromptu performances which were themselves the expression of natural instinct."

Scholars and critics have argued at considerable length as to which are the two causes referred to by Aristotle at the beginning of this passage. Are we to understand that the first of these causes is the mimetic act by which we learn our first lessons, and the second the simple intellectual pleasure which we take in a work of portrayal? If so, the difference is one between the act of creating representations and the perception of representations created by somebody else. Some critics would therefore regard it as a distinction between the creative and appreciative faculties. Others believe that the two causes are the mimetic faculty on the one hand and our inclination to harmony and rhythm on the other. But whichever we regard as Aristotle's two causes, the differentiation between mimesis on the one hand and harmony and rhythm on the other is in fact drawn. If by his "two causes" Aristotle wishes to indicate the respective pleasures of creation and appreciation, it is logical to regard harmony and rhythm in the light of a similar distinction. There must be a pleasure in creating and a pleasure in apprehending harmony and rhythm. Plato in fact actually makes this distinction, asserting that rhythm and harmony as constituted by order in movement and sound are instinctive in young human beings (*Laws* 653 e). But he also observes that the older men who are past dancing themselves may take pleasure in watching the performances of the young (*Laws* 657 d). It thus follows that, whatever we wish to understand by Aristotle's "two causes", rhythm and harmony remain distinguished from mimetic portrayal as constituting basic elements in poetry and music. If we wish to differentiate the pleasure of creation from that of appreciation, then the classificatory line will also bisect rhythm and harmony and produce a symmetrical four-cornered diagram.

In the passage which we have already quoted Aristotle refers to two kinds of mimesis which are really quite distinct, and before going any further it would be well to dispose of the first of these two kinds – which we have translated as mimicry. Indeed, the English "imitation" would serve our purposes perfectly well here, since the third kind of mimesis which refers to poetic or musical recitation is not here mentioned. When Aristotle claims that the mimetic faculty is innate in human beings and that by virtue of this faculty we learn our first lessons he is using the expression in the sense of "emulation". We learn by emulating the efforts of others. The second meaning of the term is of course that of "portrayal", a formal and intellectual appreciation of similarity in difference, which is also productive of wonder and pleasure. Here it is pertinent to quote a passage of comparable import from the *Rhetoric* (1371 b 4): "We naturally delight in works of portrayal such as painting, sculpture, and poetry, and every object that is faithfully portrayed, even though it is unattractive in itself. Thus we do not take pleasure in such objects for their own sake but because we identify them by a syllogistic process of reasoning (syllogismos) and to that extent increase our knowledge." The consistency of thought in this passage with that which we have already studied is too obvious to need comment, and it is also interesting to note the connexion between mimesis and wonder, which clearly marks artistic portrayal as an intellectual pleasure.

Mimesis as portrayal is to be discovered elsewhere in the *Poetics* and the notion underlies many of Aristotle's remarks on poetry and art. Mimesis as emulation, however, occurs nowhere else in the *Poetics*, though it certainly occurs elsewhere in Aristotelean writings. In the *Physics*, where Aristotle makes his only too well-known statement that art "imitates" Nature he means that art emulates Nature, not that it portrays Nature (*Phys.* 194 a 21). This statement has been a great source of confusion in the past. The concept of mimesis as emulation is indeed thoroughly developed in the Aristotelean canon. It is claimed (*De Mundo* 396 b 7) that art emulates Nature by availing itself of a balance of opposing forces. Just as the natural universe and human society are compounded of conflicting elements, so in the same way painting exploits colour contrasts and music reconciles divergence of pitch and time; while in writing the divergent elements are represented by vowels and consonants respectively. Art is not always content to follow Nature, but sometimes aims at surpassing her achievement. Thus in the *Politics* (1337 a 1, 2) art and education are said to make good Nature's deficiencies. Human skill may either complete what Nature has left unfinished or else reproduce Nature's processes (*Phys.* 199 a 15). The emulation of Nature is again exemplified by the art of cooking, which amounts to a kind of redigestion of food, in which the broth of the cooking-pot plays a part comparable to that of the digestive juices (*Meteor.* 381 b 6).

This theory, however, was thoroughly entrenched in Greek thought long before Aristotle's time. Democritus and Heracleitus were its spokesmen. For we read in Plutarch (*De sollert. anim.* 20. 974 a): "It is ridiculous that we should pride ourselves on powers of learning superior to those of the lower creatures, since Democritus proves that in the most important matters we are their pupils, imitating the spider in weaving and stitching, the swallow in building, and melodious birds like the swan or nightingale in song." Moreover, the passage already quoted from *De Mundo* is merely a development of Heracleitus' doctrine, and the Aristotelean writer of the treatise (who was not Aristotle himself) concludes this section of his argument by a direct appeal to the Ionian philosopher.

S. H. Butcher, in the first of his series of essays in *Aristotle's Theory of Poetry and Fine Art*, on the strength of passages which we have just cited, develops Aristotle's concept of "useful art" in connexion with the mimetic principle. Imitation in this context is clearly tantamount to emulation. Butcher then proceeds (in the second essay) to examine imitation in its sense of artistic representation or reproduction (i.e. portrayal), though he is anxious to assure us at the outset that there is no question of "a literal transcript of the world of reality". The distinction, however, between useful and fine art is no sooner made than blurred, for Butcher argues that the poet, in Aristotle's opinion, aims at portraying the world not as it is, but better than it is. In support of this view he is able to appeal to an important passage in the *Poetics* (1460 b 6):

"The number and nature of critical problems and the solution to them will be clear if we take the following facts into account. The poet is as much concerned to portray life as he who paints and models it; and it follows that there are three aspects of life which he may portray: life, that is, in the light of present or past fact, of reputation, and of propriety."[1] This last phrase, literally rendered, gives us: "things as they were or are, as men say they are or as they seem, or as they ought to be." While still on the same subject Aristotle remarks a little further on: "The objection that a work is not true to fact, may in some cases be countered by the retort that it answers to our aspirations (is as it ought to be). Thus Sophocles claimed that his creations had regard to propriety, Euripides' only to fact; and this would seem a fair contention. Again, in some cases, as happens in fables of the gods, both our credulity and our sense of propriety is flouted; yet there remains an appeal to tradition. The narrative is neither an improvement on fact nor true to it, and may even be all that Xenophanes says of such nar-

---

[1] The translation given here is independent of Butcher's.

ratives; nevertheless we are excused by conformity to a traditional account. Or yet again, when the plea of propriety cannot be advanced, ancient custom may vindicate us. An instance is the description of the weapons in the *Iliad*: 'The spears stood upright on their butt-ends.' That was the normal practice of the times and it remains such among the Illyrians today."

Aristotle is here dealing with captious critics who find the scenes described by the poet objectionable because these lie outside their own limited experience. Elsewhere, he meets objections on the ground of impossibility with the same kind of defence. The poetic rendering of life may be justified on grounds of propriety or traditional opinion, literally, "because it is better or according to opinion". The objection of impossibility, Aristotle tells us, was brought against Zeuxis' painting, but the painter claimed that his work was superior to actuality and that the painter's model should transcend common experience (or that the painter should improve upon his model) (1461 b 9).

From these statements Butcher extracts the following doctrine: "The general movement of organic life is part of a progress to the 'better', the several parts working together for the good of the whole. The artist in his mimic world carries forward this movement to a more perfect completion. The creations of his art are framed on those ideal lines that Nature has drawn: her intimations, her guidance are what he follows. He too aims at something better than the actual. He produces a new thing, not the actual thing of experience, not a copy of reality, but a 'better' or higher reality – 'for the ideal type must surpass the actual'; the ideal is better than the real."

Yet the artist, according to Aristotle, may or may not portray life as it ought to be. Other courses are open to him. Emulation, it is true, aims at an ideal, but not portrayal. Not only aspiration but fact or reputation may be the artist's guide. By the phrase "for the ideal type must surpass

H

the actual" Butcher is translating the argument quoted in favour of Zeuxis – that the painter's work must improve on experience. We should prefer to translate the whole relevant passage as follows:

"The charge of impossibility in general must be viewed in the light of poetic effect, human aspirations, or a traditional account. As regards poetic effect, it is better for a story to be convincing at the expense of possibility than vice-versa. Again, it may be alleged that characters are not true to life, like the figures painted by Zeuxis. We may answer, however, that such creations excel life, for in this type of work the model itself must exhibit excellence."

The statement that art *must* excel life is only applicable to the art of Zeuxis and painters who employed a similar style, for Aristotle tells us earlier in the *Poetics* (1448 a 5) that artists vary in this respect thus: "Polygnotus selected models of superior type, Pauson inferior; while Dionysius portrayed average persons. Clearly, each mode of literary portrayal will exhibit the same distinction and will become a separate genre in so far as the models on which it bases itself fall into one of the above distinct categories." It is also worth remembering that Zeuxis was the painter of whom the story is told by Cicero and Pliny that he made selective use of several models in order to produce an ideal of feminine beauty. In this case the superiority of the artist's work was due to calculated selection, not to any visionary insight into Nature's purpose, such as Butcher's interpretation suggests. The truth is that Butcher is trying to reconcile Aristotle with Hegel, as we become increasingly aware when he attributes to Aristotle the view that a work of art is "an idealized representation of human life – of character, emotion, and action – under forms manifest to sense."

For Aristotle, however, there is an essential correspondence between a work of art and the experience of the public for which it is destined. The experience of individuals of course varies, and Aristotle is at pains to point out

that his notion of mimesis allows for higher or lower types
of character, more or less exalted planes of action, differences of fashion or local custom, variations in tradition, and
discrepancies in report, as well as actual errors in minor
details of fact which may or may not be justified by the
circumstances (1460 b 15). Consequently, since art bears
reference to general, not individual experience, it selects its
material from general, not individual experience, and in
this respect it shows itself a more philosophical and higher
study than history (1451 b 5), for it considers *possible* com-
binations of circumstance, not particular; and as we have
seen in the *Metaphysics* Aristotle regarded the ability to
arrive at generalities through particular experience the
essence of philosophic power. Indeed, art, so regarded,
seems to combine both the inductive and deductive faculties; for observation of particulars leads the artist to certain
conclusions about general possibility – an induction – while
his actual work is a particular possibility deduced to be
plausible on the basis of his general inductions.

Nevertheless, the relation of art to experience is every-
where stressed. The relationship is a formal one, an example of variety in difference. Mimesis is a principle of
external form, corresponding to a principle of internal form
implied in the size and proportion of the work and in the
arrangement of its parts (1451 a 4, 1450 b 23). If this, then,
is Aristotle's concept of mimesis in the *Poetics*, why does he
preface his remarks on the subject with a reference to that
other kind of mimesis which we interpret by the word
"emulation"? The trouble is that the *Poetics* seems uncertain at several points as to whether it wishes to be what is
claimed at the outset, a treatise on poetry, or whether it is
to take the form of an answer in debating style to Plato's
challenge in the tenth book of the *Republic*. The reference to
the mimetic faculty in respect of emulation is clearly made
with Plato in mind. Plato damned poetry because it was
mimetic. Aristotle argues that mimesis is not necessarily

bad, and to dispose of prejudice he initially selects one aspect of it which is obviously good – the instinct for emulation which stimulates the acquisition of most human skills. If this kind of mimesis is good, why not the more complicated kind of poetic mimesis with its meaning of "portrayal"? There is nothing inherently derogatory in the word and its cognate forms, and in any case Aristotle did not believe in the Theory of Ideas to which Plato had mainly appealed in his denigration of the mimetic artist.

At the same time, there is not absolute consistency in Aristotle's use of the mimetic vocabulary to denote a formal and intellectual process such as warrants the translation "portrayal". We have already alluded to a third, particularly Greek application of the word "mimeisthai" which was applied to poetic recitation and to performances of music and dancing. The modern Swiss scholar H. Koller has insisted very strongly on this meaning of the word in his work *Die Mimesis in der Antike*. Aristotle himself was quite aware of the distinction, and at the outset of the *Poetics* (1447 a 22) he classifies those arts which represent life through rhythm, speech, and tune, segregating them carefully from the inert arts which make use of form and colour. Rhythm alone, he adds, even without the aid of tonality can imitate dispositions of mind, emotions, and actions – as it does in dancing; and the distinction between such representations and those of the inert arts is made clearer in the *Politics* (1340 a 35), where he argues that in painting representations of character are effected indirectly through sense impressions, whereas in music they are direct. Rhythms and tunes reproduce in the hearer anger and gentleness, courage and restraint with all their opposite corresponding qualities (1340 a 19). None of this is very clearly expressed, but it is not difficult to see what Aristotle is driving at. The inert arts depend more upon the organs of sense, which in so far as they furnish the *clearest* (not necessarily most powerful) impressions of our experience, are the servants of our rational faculties. The progressive arts, whose fleeting and fluid nature does not admit of study and analysis, make their attack rather upon the nerves, and the emotional effects which they reproduce in us are achieved without reference to the brain. On deep analysis, even wordless music of the most formal type could probably be shown to make its effect through a subconscious relationship with our experience of life. The difference between this and pictorial mimesis is the difference between a rational and irrational faculty. Moreover, a certain rhythm or melody, a certain tonality, rhythm, or musical interval will produce in the hearer a muscular tension or relaxation which could be equally produced by a wide variety of external sense impressions. The musical effect indeed reproduces the experience of life, but it reproduces it internally at a nervous and muscular level,[1] while painting creates a situation which in turn produces a thought, which finally produces the nervous or muscular reaction. The indirect method is clearer, the direct more powerful.

These last considerations lead us naturally from the question of mimesis to that of rhythm. Let us see if it is possible to discover a rational and irrational, conscious and subconscious aspect of the same phenomenon. The *Poetics* tells us very little about Aristotle's view of rhythm and in order to find a longer statement on the subject we are obliged to consult the *Rhetoric*:

"The form of rhetorical diction is neither metrical on the one hand nor devoid of rhythm on the other. Metre does not carry conviction; it is too manifestly artificial; at the same time it exerts an irrational appeal (literally: 'produces ecstasy') in the sense that we are alert to its responsions and anticipate its recurrences. . . . The unrhythmic is the indeterminate. The form of diction thus must be

---

[1] Perhaps also "glandular"!

determined – but not by metre. The indeterminate appeals neither to taste nor intelligence. All phenomena are determined by number, and rhythm is the numerical aspect of form in diction; from which metre is a separable element. It follows that a speech must have rhythm but not metre, since metre would make it a poem. Even the rhythm must not be too precise; it is permissible only up to a certain point." (*Rhet.* 1408 b 21 ff.)

We have already noticed the correspondence between rhythm in the arts of progressive media and form in inert media. Tonality and rhythm reproduce mental dispositions independent of any rational responson to experience. In the above passage, however, rhythm appears to be almost equated with form, and we should not be surprised at this, for in the *Metaphysics* (985 b 13) Aristotle in fact identifies form with rhythm. The atomic theory of Democritus and Leucippus is under discussion, and Aristotle is concerned to explain the quaint Ionic dialect of these early philosophers in terms which his Athenian contemporaries will understand. Atoms according to the Ionian theory are conditioned in three respects: shape, order, and position. The Ionic word for shape is "rhysmos" (i.e. rhythmos) and Aristotle declares that this is what is meant by "schema", the ordinary Athenian word for form. Defined thus as the equivalent of form, rhythm is obviously a rational element. This concept is peculiarly Greek, for western usage tends to stress the irrational aspects of rhythm. Aristides Quintilianus, a musical theorist of late but uncertain date, writes:

"Rhythm has three meanings. It is said to exist in inert bodies, in the sense that a statue may display a rhythmic grace. Secondly, it belongs to moving objects, so that we describe a man as walking rhythmically. Especially, however, it applies to sound, the aspect which here interests us. A mere assembly of notes in irregular progression would deprive musical texture of any emphasis and perplex the mind, but rhythmic structure makes clear the force of the melody, allotting the time and imparting to the intelligence orderly impulses."[1]

It is interesting to notice that this identification of rhythm with formal order and regulation persists throughout the whole history of the Greek language. Thus in Byzantine Greek the "idiorhythma" denote monasteries in which monks live apart, each following his own *rule*, as distinct from the "koinobia" where a communal discipline is strongly enforced. In modern Greek "rhythmos" applies not only to a classical order of architecture but may be used of architectural style in general (e.g. "Gothic rhythm"). Now, this rational and formal concept of rhythm is not only foreign to our own western notion but even provokes some writers on the subject to contemptuous repudiation. Let us take examples:

"Rhythm is not mere time or metre. Jazz, popularly supposed to be much the most rhythmic music, is not rhythmic at all, but rigidly metrical. True rhythm has the fundamental regularity, but also the quick responsive variability, of the human pulse, not the mechanically precise beat of the metronome. It feels time and goes in time, but not dead in time."[2]

While the writer concedes the principle of time and regularity he is concerned to assert that of variability, and metre so far from being included as an aspect of rhythm (as Aristotle has it) appears almost in contrast to it. Musical rhythm is the theme of these remarks, but a writer on poetry discusses the nature of rhythm in very much the same spirit:

"A misconception about rhythm (poetic) . . . is that which neatly and too exclusively relates it to other kinds of rhythm such as the beating of the heart, the motion of the arms and legs in walking, the alternation of day and night,

---

[1] Translated from *Die Fragmente und die Lehrsätze der Griecheschen Rhythmiker*, von Rudolf Westphal, Teubner, 1861, p. 47.
[2] Eric Blom in *The Musical Companion*, ed. Bacharach, Gollancz, 1934.

of the seasons, the moon's passage round the earth, the earth's round the sun. . . ."[1]

The writer further observes that such mistaken accounts of rhythm omit "real emphasis". The concept of rhythm as a principle of variety in rebellion against the rigidity of metre is even more strongly marked than in the previous quotation. The Greek view of rhythm, however, was not purely formal and rational, and though it laid stress on an aspect which we tend to neglect or deprecate, it did not entirely neglect or deprecate those aspects which we stress. This is abundantly clear in Aristotle's account of rhythm in the *Rhetoric*. For he states that a certain degree of rhythm is necessary in order to foster an irrational elation in the audience – that is, to produce "ecstasy" (1408 b 35). Metre is to be avoided because its irrational potentiality is too great (1400 b 22). Here, however, we seem to strike a difficulty, for we are told almost in the same breath that metre is too artificial or mechanical. How are we to interpret a statement which attributes to the same practice an excess both of calculation and of passion? Yet this statement succinctly summarizes our problem. How do two conceptions, one essentially rational, the other irrational, come to be associated under the single term "rhythm"? Now, although Aristotle admits the irrational content of rhythm and metre, he is much more explicit concerning its formal and rational aspects, so that our best course will be to examine his concept of form in the hope that the irrational elements in rhythm will reveal themselves by contrast or inference.

Aristotle's notion of form depends primarily upon a concept of part and whole, unit and component. The simplest statement of this view occurs in the *Politics* where the composition of the Greek city state is under discussion. "A league (or alliance)", he says, "is one thing and a city another. The former is a matter of strength in numbers,

[1] H. Coombes, *Literature and Criticism in Writing*, Chatto and Windus, 1953.

homogeneous as it is. It exists solely for support, as a kind of makeweight. But the components of a unit must be heterogeneous." (1261 a 24) In the *Poetics*, dramatic form is conceived as tripartite, consisting of a beginning, middle, and end. Each part differs from the other in quality (as the various social elements in the city state differ). Thus the beginning must be without cause, the end without result, while the middle must possess both cause and result. The whole is thus rendered coherent and at the same time isolated by the very nature of its parts, so that Aristotle is further able to assert: "The parts (of dramatic action) must cohere so intimately that their transposal or withdrawal will result in the deformation and dislocation of the whole, for any factor which by its presence does not contribute to the definition of the whole constitutes no part of it." (1451 a 30)

In the same context, however (1451 a 34), a further principle of form is proclaimed. Form, in order that the mind may readily accommodate it, must assume a magnitude such as the capacity of our senses dictates. Thus we have the well-known statement that a beautiful object is of moderate size such as may readily be entertained by the eye, and in the same way a narrative must be of a length which the memory may easily grasp (1451 a 4). Indeed, the size of the whole, like the disposition of the parts, must contribute to the definition of the work (1451 a 35). As long as these formal conditions are satisfied we may apply the rule of "the bigger the better" (1451 a 9). The same principle is also stated in the *Rhetoric* (1409 b 1) where Aristotle prescribes the character of a good prose period: "By a period I mean that which has a self-determined beginning and end, and an extent which the vision can readily entertain." That is to say, the position of beginning and end must be fixed by content, not only magnitude; for such is the meaning of self-determined. The limits are not imposed merely by external contingency but are vital parts of the period itself. Such a period is formally preferable to the earlier kind of prose style, which was loose rather than periodic.

Aristotle's remarks must here be understood in relation to his discussion of form in the *Metaphysics* (1078 b 2), where the term "limit" is to be identified with magnitude, and proportion (symmetria) concerns the inter-relation of the parts and their organization in the whole. The magnitude of a work besides being determined by our senses or memory is also prescribed by function. This is made clear also in the *Poetics*: "The extent of a work will be adequately determined if it allows for the probable or necessary stages which accompany the character's transition from adverse to favourable fortune or the contrary process." (1451 a 12)

Proportion, it appears, is largely a matter of precedent and itself implies a question of magnitude – the magnitude not of the whole but of the part; for the size of one part raises expectation as regards the size of another. As Aristotle observes, we expect recurrences in verse metre; and a quantitative precedent operates in physical and social units. In the *Politics*, apropos of dangerous excrescences in the community, he writes: "A body is composed of parts and its development must conform to the requirements of proportion. Otherwise, it deteriorates, as in the instance of a leg four cubits long appended to a body of two spans. In some cases a creature might be transformed from its proper nature into that of another simply by a quantitatively disproportionate development. A city is composed of parts in the same way. . . ." (1302 b 35)

If, however, we turn from these formal concepts which are connected with the idea of rhythm to the metaphor inherent in the word, the full range of its meaning becomes apparent. Rhythm means "flow" and is derived from the verb which means "to flow". This aspect of rhythm was investigated by Otto Shröder in the German classical review *Hermes* (1918). Shröder considers a fragment of Archilochus in which the human soul is represented as storm-tossed amid the billows of varying fortune. There is here a clear analogy between the rhythm of human life and that of the waves. Yet rhythm is not simply a question of rise and fall but also of current and direction. In Greek, the word sometimes seems to be applied simply to the rise and fall of the waves of the sea, but the truth is that the Greeks regarded the Ocean as a river, and the Bosphorus was similarly regarded. When Greek poets refer to the "flow" of these seas, they are thinking not only of undulation but of current, and the Greek idea of rhythm is one of current combined with alternation, of continuity with vicissitude.

It is now possible to see how the notion of rhythm is both similar and dissimilar to that of form. There is regularity and proportion in the units of rhythm; the crests and the troughs of the waves represent a symmetrical deviation on either side of an undisturbed level. But the metaphor is from the river not the sea, and the ends of the river, its source and its mouth, are both out of sight. There is no proportion between the size of the parts and the seemingly infinite size of the whole. Rhythm is like "a leg four cubits long appended to a body of two spans". Again, we may consider the whole river as a meandering line on the map, clearly differentiated from the features of the surrounding terrain, that is to say, formally distinct as a whole. But just as the whole seems infinite when we consider the parts, so the parts, the single fluctuations, seem infinitesimal when we turn our attention to the whole. There is no proportionate relation between part and whole. In this way series differs from form, although it possesses many formal characteristics; series is form with one element lacking.

Now, everybody knows that series is hypnotic. Counting sheep is a time-honoured remedy for insomnia. It would seem that our rational powers are captured by the formal and rational aspects of series only to be frustrated and stultified, once captured. There is analogy between the hypnotic power of series and rhythm on the one hand and the bewildering effect of Aristotle's "wonder" on the other. In each case reason leads us to bewilderment, but in rhythm and series the effect is achieved subconsciously, so that the feeling of stupefaction and hypnosis is immediate without any sense of initial stimulation of the rational faculties. It is easy to see how in Aristotle wonder is associated with form (including mimesis) but "ecstasy" and "enthusiasm" are produced by rhythmic effects. At the same time we can now explain how Aristotle regards metre as something artificial and calculated as well as hypnotic and "enthusiastic". The moment-to-moment oscillations of long and short, or strong and weak syllables represent the undulant and fluctuating aspect of rhythm, productive of hypnotic effect. In an epic poem the recurrence of metrical patterns in the form of lines results in a series comparable to a continuous succession of regular vibrations on a steadily moving surface. As such, the line unit, like the syllable unit, is an irrational and mesmeric element. But in a small poem the line assumes a comparative magnitude which makes it a rationally appre-hended part of the whole. It thus becomes a formal, not a hypnotic ingredient, and the same rule of course applies with much greater force to extensive stanzas and strophes constructed on a complex metrical pattern. They are numerable and recognizable parts of a whole, not an infini-tude of dimples upon its surface. When Aristotle tells us, as he does, that metre is the "numerable aspect of the spoken form" (*Rhet.* 1408 b 26) he is clearly thinking of metre in its architectural capacity.

At the beginning of the *Poetics* (1447 a 15–29) Aristotle carefully distinguishes the progressive arts from the inert. The former make use of rhythm, language, and tonality, whereas the medium of the latter is colour and form. Here, rhythm is not considered as a formal but a fluctuating and bewildering power in sharp contrast to rational form. In fact, its very fluctuating and incalculable nature make it the natural medium for reproducing the fluctuating moods and

dispositions of the human "psyche". Poetry, and especially
dramatic poetry, stands midway between the arts of static
and fluctuating media. Its affinities with music are obvious
and there is equally no question of its power to create images
and pictures in the mind. Hence Aristotle regards it as being based on mimesis or representation as well as upon
rhythm and tonality. The question naturally occurs to us:
is there an irrational element implied in the formality of
the inert arts corresponding to the rational aspects of
metre and rhythm which we have just investigated? An
appeal to experience will at once secure the answer "yes".
In later European art the hypnotic potentiality of painting
is considerable. Homogeneity in lighting and colour selection
is the spacial equivalent of series and rhythm in time. The
Greeks, however, disposed only of few colours and simple
colour effects, and it is doubtful if they were able to suggest or insinuate passions and dispositions of mind so subtly
as does the modern artist. Nevertheless, there is a rhythmic
grace of line present in Greek sculpture which is analogous
to musical rhythm and has nothing to do with formal and
rational harmonies. Similarly, in a drawing, the movement
of the artist's hand may be felt in the quality of his line,
precisely as a dance movement is felt. In such aspects of the
inert arts we discover an irrational and hypnotic power.
The truth is that these arts are not so inert as they at first
seem, in so far as the muscular energy of the artist is felt in
the art. Nor did this less obvious quality of painting and
sculpture escape Aristotle. In the *Politics* he observed:
"The other objects of sense experience (i.e. non-aural experience) cannot represent character. This is quite evident
when we consider touch and taste. In visual perceptions,
forms possess some slight potentiality of this sort, though it
is not felt by everybody". (1340 a 29) He goes on to say
that visual arts convey emotions indirectly through forms
and colours which betoken the presence of such emotions.
This is of course a different matter. Everybody understands

the meaning of an angry or sorrowful gesture. But when Aristotle speaks of visual forms possessing an emotional potency comparable to that of music, such as is not felt by everybody, it seems probable that he is thinking of subtle rhythmic linear effects analogous to the flow of dance or song.

CHAPTER VII

Catharsis

It is disconcerting after art and poetry have been defined in terms of mimesis and rhythm to be introduced at a later stage in the *Poetics* to a new notion in the form of "catharsis" or purification, to which our pleasure in tragic performance is apparently attributed. Even if we did not possess the incomplete eighth book of the *Politics* the term would at first sight seem to represent a fundamental idea in the theory of poetry and art as a whole, not merely a function peculiar to tragedy. For assuming that it were peculiar to tragedy, we should naturally be led to expect the differentiation of comedy and other genres by the use of other analogous terms, and no such terms are to be discovered in Aristotle's work. On the contrary, pity and fear, through which the tragic catharsis is effected, obviously suggest themselves as tragic differentiae and seem to hint at a catharsis which might be effected through other emotions in other genres of poetic art. Moreover, the relevant passage in the *Politics* is quite conclusive evidence that catharsis was not conceived by Aristotle as a peculiarity of dramatic practice but was also the professed function of certain types of music. The fact that cathartic purpose was attributable only to certain specific kinds of music might lead us to suspect that it was similarly attributable only to certain specific kinds of poetry. Nevertheless, a principle which manifests itself in two domains as clearly distinguishable as music and drama would appear to be rooted in impulses which underly a very wide field of artistic expression. Aristotle, however, has already confronted us with two radical principles (mimesis and rhythm), on the basis of which all music and literary art seem explicable. It is important to discover whether catharsis supplements these principles in some significant way or whether it is merely a redundant notion – the fragment perhaps of a discarded theory. At the same time, a term such as catharsis with its purificatory or clarificatory implications suggests some degree of moral or rational amelioration, such as might well mark the *end* as distinct from the *process* of art. This distinction we discovered in our study of Plato's aesthetic concepts, and it is also important in our understanding of Aristotle. Like Plato, Aristotle calls attention to the hypnotic and fascinating power of poetry, and like Plato he seems to demand that this power shall be exercised in pursuit of a moral or rational end. As to the relation between the fascinating and elevating capacity of poetry and art Plato seems never quite to have satisfied himself. What could poetry do that philosophy could not do better? This doubt presented itself to Plato's mind because his notion of philosophy was inextricably associated with the person of Socrates – with whom he was in the deepest sense "in love". Poetry was a kind of love inferior to philosophy; and perhaps it is true that he who has a Socrates does not need poetry and art. For Aristotle, however, Socrates was a philosopher among philosophers. Aristotle's clearer thought and less ardent nature did not dispose him to hero-worship, and for this very reason he was better qualified than Plato to understand how in certain circumstances a poet may be a useful substitute for a saint.

We shall do best to begin by a consideration of Aristotle's remarks on music in the *Politics*. Since the German scholars, Weil and Bernays, drew attention to this passage some hundred years ago it has been customary to explain the catharsis referred to in the *Poetics* by allusion to the *Politics*. It should be remembered, however, that Aristotle in fact refers us from the *Politics* to the *Poetics*, and this is surely the correct order in which to approach the subject. Furthermore, our knowledge of Greek music is negligible. Of Greek poetry the same cannot be said. To appeal from the *Poetics* to the musical catharsis described in the *Politics* is therefore to interpret the more comprehensible in terms of the less. The contrary procedure is obviously preferable. We must first form certain general notions from the *Politics* and then consult the *Poetics* for clearer definition.

The discussion of music in the *Politics* follows that of gymnastics (1339 a 11), perhaps because the two activities were dealt with in adjacent contexts by Plato in the *Republic*. Aristotle deliberates concerning the various possible uses or purposes assignable to music. Do we indulge in music merely for amusement? Or is it to be cultivated in the interests of education, forming character as gymnastics form the body? Or again, is it the occupation of a serious and cultured adult's leisure hours? Aristotle characteristically concedes that life has a place even for idle amusement. Music is light-heartedly associated with unambitious pleasures in the phrase "sleeping, drinking, and music"; with which we may compare our own expression "wine, women, and song". Music, however, was an essential part of Greek education, and any activity approached in such a light-hearted spirit could hardly qualify for a place in serious school studies. Some modern educationists would do well to notice Aristotle's remark in this context: one does not play while learning – learning is painful. Nor can the place of music in the syllabus be justified as a training for the more serious and adult employment of leisure, since technical instruction for such a purpose is unnecessary; the Persian kings and the Spartans were both reputed to appreciate music even though they had no knowledge of its technique and themselves disdained to perform. The question therefore arises as to whether music should be retained in the curriculum; and its retention can only be fully justified by the justification of pleasure. Pleasure is, after all, a form of relaxation, a release from toil and pain. Admittedly,

I

human beings often regard pleasure as an end in itself, whereas relaxation does not constitute such an end. Nevertheless, this attitude is not completely inconsistent, for pleasure may be regarded as an immediate end, which in some way supports the remoter end (i.e. the end implied in those activities for which recreation refreshes and re-equips us). But pleasure alone is not enough to justify the teaching of music. Music is capable of affording a more refined type of enjoyment, and as such may influence the character in process of entertaining.

To the passage which follows these observations we have already referred. In it Aristotle draws distinctions between musical and pictorial art. Then comes a discussion of the emotional values of the different modes or tonalities employed by Greek music, with the important allusion to catharsis:

"Accepting the distinction made by some philosophers as between ethical, active, and hypnotic (enthusiastic) melodies and the assignment of these different types to their respectively appropriate modes, let us add that music is to be valued not for one but for several of the effects which it is capable of producing. For instance, it may serve for purificatory and educational purposes. The term 'purification', of which we make use in passing, will be explained more fully in our work on *Poetry*. There is, moreover, yet a third type of music which may occupy our leisure, providing relaxation and relief from strain. Since each purpose is admissible, all modes are of service, providing they are properly used. That is to say: the ethical modes are valuable as exercises in education, but the active and hypnotic ones, while we may listen to them ourselves, should be left to other exponents. Mental disturbances, which are pathological in some cases, afflict all of us in reduced or acute measure. Thus we find pity and fear in the former instance and pathological disorders in the latter. Persons who are a prey to such disorders are seen to be restored when they listen to the delirious strains of sacred song, just as though they had been medically treated and purged. In precisely the same way, pity, fear, and other such emotions, in so far as they affect each of us, will yield to the purificatory effect and pleasurable relief produced by music. In fact, there is an element of harmless pleasure even in the melodies of specifically purificatory purpose."

The word which we translate by "pathological disorders" is "enthousiasmos". The "hypnotic" melodies are "enthousiastica", and it is evident from this that "enthusiasm" is considered both as a cure and as a disease. Aristotle is describing a homoeopathic cure. Pity and fear seem to be identified with the minor forms of mental disturbance and "enthusiasm" with more serious manifestations. The first reference to catharsis has been translated as "purification", but further down the word "purged" has been used to bring out the medical analogy. There has been a great deal of controversy as to whether the inherent metaphor in catharsis is medical or religious. It is clear, however, from the passage in the *Politics* that Aristotle was conscious of both medical and religious analogies when he used the word. Persons who suffer from pity and fear in a mild degree are compared to those violent sufferers who are benefited by the frenzy of exotic religious rites and the sacred songs connected with them. These in turn remind him of patients who by taking medicine are purged and restored to physical equilibrium. Indeed, the history of the word "catharsis" makes it quite natural that both analogies should have suggested themselves to Aristotle. The priests had originally combined healing with their religious functions, and though it is true that Greek scientific medicine had evolved independently of these semi-religious cures, the religious and scientific associations of the word undoubtedly merged in Pythagorean doctrine. The term was also used in connexion with the Orphic and Eleusinian mystery rites, and through the former probably influenced Socrates, accounting for the beliefs expressed in the *Phaedo*, where it indicates a state in which the soul is freed from the trammels of material existence and is so prepared to enter upon a sublime immortality (*Phaed.* 67 b).

In Greek music, then, and possibly in all music, we are to understand that mental stability is attained through a kind of hypnotism which is reflected in medical and religious analogy. The question remains how far this analogy is to be carried. Does it, for instance, imply some kind of expulsion or separation? Morbid elements in the soul are naturally expelled by any healing process, but beyond that the analogy does not much help us. Modern commentators have inferred that music and poetry release emotion by giving it a harmless outlet, and as a result Aristole has been made responsible for precisely such a doctrine. The Loeb editor of the *Politics* even asserts in a footnote that "in *Poetics* c. vi tragedy is said to purge the emotions of pity and fear by giving them an outlet". Yet the text of the *Poetics* does not warrant the word "outlet" or anything which resembles it. The idea is an interpolation.

It is true that Aristotle regarded some kinds of music as an outlet. Music, he claims (*Pol.* 1340 b 28), may keep boys harmlessly occupied, in the same way that a rattle amuses an infant. Young people – an echo of Plato's *Laws* – cannot keep still, and music gives orderly expression to their energy. Aristotle, however, is in this passage thinking only of children's education and the reference is to musical performance, not appreciation. The very fact that he advances such an idea in connexion with education proves conclusively that it was not fundamental in his view of catharsis; for cathartic music in the *Politics* is sharply distinguished from educational music. It uses different modes and different instruments. For example, the flute is suitable for catharsis rather than instruction (1341 a 23) and Plato is blamed for having classed the Phrygian mode with the Dorian as educational (*Pol.* 1342 a 34, cf. *Rep.* 399 a). It is really an excitable mode like those used by religious music in effecting its cathartic purpose.

Apart, however, from considerations based on study of the text, the very notion that morbid passions may be exorcised simply by giving them expression is psychologically false; and to attribute such an idea to Aristotle is an affront to the memory of one who was a penetrating psychologist. S. H. Butcher gives us a statement of the case such as still meets with wide acceptance:

"Plato, it must be remembered, in his attack upon the drama, had said that 'the natural hunger after sorrow and weeping' which is kept under control in our own calamities is satisfied and delighted by the poets. 'Poetry feeds and waters the passions instead of starving them.' Through its tearful moods it enfeebles the manly temper; it makes anarchy in the soul by exalting the lower elements over the higher, and by dethroning reason in favour of feeling. Aristotle held that it is not desirable to kill or to starve the emotional part of the soul, and that the regulated indulgence of the feelings serves to maintain the balance of our nature. Tragedy, he would say, is a vent for the particular emotions of pity and fear. In the first instance, it is true, its effect is not to tranquillize but to excite. It excites emotion, however, only to allay it. Pity and fear, artificially stirred, expel the latent pity and fear which we bring with us from real life, or at least, such elements in them as are disquieting. In the pleasurable calm which follows when passion is spent, an emotional cure has been wrought."

It is only fair to observe at once that Butcher is here expounding Bernays' view rather than his own. He himself insists that the emotions of pity and fear are not so much expelled as transformed and are "transmuted into higher and more refined forms". He also quotes Galen and Plato to prove that the medical catharsis indicates the removal of morbid, not superfluous, matter, the word "kenosis" being reserved for the latter process. No psychiatric process can

be dissociated entirely from moral standards, but the cathartic process, as described in the *Politics*, obviously raises
psychological questions, and Butcher's terminology is possibly too redolent of morality. Thus he tells us that fear
through its alliance with pity is "divested of narrow selfishness". The result of tragedy is a "noble emotional satisfaction". The spectator is "brought face to face with universal law and the divine plan of the world". To credit
poetry and drama with such motives is to make them tres-
passers in the domain of religion, and perhaps for this
reason Butcher's arguments have not received the sympathy which they in some ways deserved; for Butcher was
groping after a theory essentially saner than that which
Bernays had attributed to Aristotle. For instance, Butcher's
use of the word "selfish" may well have been prompted
by psychological considerations, though he himself is confused by the moral associations of the word and its equation
in colloquial language with greed or ambition. An aesthetic
experience indeed deprives us of selfishness in the sense that
it reduces our self-consciousness, which in most persons is
too oppressive to admit the re-adjustments which life con-
stantly demands of them. Butcher, however, should have
pointed out that in shedding such "selfishness" we also
abandon our sense of responsibility and duty together with
that of self-interest and ambition. An amoral dissociation
from self must be achieved before a moral, altruistic unsel-
fishness can be suggested.

The cathartic experience, then, is obviously both hypnotic and moral. It is psychiatric. The difference between the
religious and medical view – so much debated – is not really
important, since the fundamental notion is one of amelioration under hypnotism, but if the point be pressed it would
seem that, paradoxically, Aristotle's view of "religious"
catharsis is medical, while his concept of artistic catharsis
is religious (subject to reservations suggested in the last
paragraph). For he clearly indicates that the catharsis of

the sacred songs caters for psychopaths, while the cathartic elements of ordinary music are a relief to ordinary people in whom anxiety states are not so strongly pronounced. The difference between religious and medical psychology is to be found in a different concept of normality. To the medical man normal mentality is average mentality. To a religious view, the normal is the ideal and the average is psychopathic (cf. the notion of fallen nature). The ancient mystery rites, at any rate temporarily, seem to have relieved persons who were not only sub-normal in the religious sense, but sub-average in the medical sense. Music as an art, however, according to Aristotle's theory, raises us from the average to the ideal. In claiming the function of art as religious, of course, we do not identify art with religion, for art is distinguished not only by its religious (i.e. rational and moral) function but by its hypnotic process – which it does not possess in common with religion, unless by "religion" we mean Corybantic dancing or other barbarous rites in which higher concepts of morality and rationality are sacrificed to mesmeric power.

Here then is a view of catharsis which amounts not to a discharge but a sublimation of emotion, achieved under some fascinating or hypnotic influence. This interestingly corresponds to Plato's concept of sublimated erotic passion, which he himself compares (in the *Phaedrus*) to poetic inspiration. We may now approach the famous definition of tragedy in the *Poetics* (1449 b 24) which has been debated word by word ever since Bernays re-opened it as a ground for controversy one century ago. Let us set Aristotle's definition before us:

"Tragedy is the portrayal of an exalted action, which forms a complete entity and is of specific duration. The language is attractively elaborated; and its elaborations are distributed according to kind among the various parts of the play. It is acted, not recited; and it uses pity and fear to effect the catharsis of these very same emotions."

A vast number of other renderings of course exist. By-water lists fifty-five translations into various European languages at the end of his 1909 edition, and since then translations, editions, and commentaries on the *Poetics* have been steadily accumulating. The above interpretation, however, is the basis on which we now intend to argue. It would appear that there are two ingredients in the cathartic process. One of these is the excitement of pity and fear. The other is the essential "goodness" of the characters who contributed to an "exalted" action. The word which we have translated as "exalted" could be more faithfully represented with a phrase such as "an action of consequence", but since this is cumbersome we shall content ourselves with a warning that such "exaltation" must be understood in an intellectual and even social, as well as a moral sense – in the widest possible sense in fact. Now, the characters, as Aristotle tells us, are implied in the action (1450 a 21), though he admits that they express themselves through what they say, not only through what they do (1454 a 18). By "goodness" Aristotle does not mean *only* the submissive virtues because he is at pains to point out that he includes them in the term "good". Thus even a woman or slave may be good, though in another sense the former is inferior and the latter utterly worthless (1454 a 20). The explanation is necessary because to the Greeks virtue meant primarily public virtue and only secondarily private virtue. The "aristoi" in a Greek state were the best men in the sense that they were the leading men – not the saints! Our modern usage implies the reverse attitude, but Aristotle's remark is not entirely out of date; for even in an age when women indignantly refuse to be the servants or subjects of men, they often relish a position as a man's second-in-command more than command itself.

Broadly speaking, the Greek word which we translate in this context as "good", like that which we have rendered "exalted", is such as to include all moral, intellectual, or social superiority. This consideration will help us to understand Aristotle's insistence on the necessity for some weakness or failing in the noble tragic character (1453 a 10). When he tells us that the tragic sufferer is some lofty personality like Oedipus or Thyestes overthrown by a failing in his character, we assume that the failing is moral, the essential goodness at least partly social. On the other hand, in a character like Antigone the essential goodness is moral. Her weakness is social; she is a woman (inferior if not utterly worthless!!). In later European drama it is particularly true that tragic interest does not always centre in the title character. This possibly is due to a greater number of characters in the play, though the "confidants" in French classic drama must be discounted as an equivalent of the Greek chorus, a device for conveying thoughts which in narrative would be recorded as unspoken. However that may be, Corneille certainly claimed in a critical preface that he had dispensed with the prescription of Aristotle in so far as he had not kept Polyeucte within the limits of a "médiocre bonté". Perhaps the tragic power of the play is explicable on the same grounds as that of Sophocles' *Antigone*: the protagonist is at a social disadvantage. But again, it would be possible to regard the tragic sufferers as comprising not the saint himself but the other characters of "médiocre bonté" who endure the overwhelming embarrassment of sanctity in their midst.

The point of Aristotle's stipulation about the tragic weakness or failing is that the tragic sufferer must be vulnerable. While he is "good", while we admire him, and while we recognize that his sufferings are unmerited or at any rate in excess of his merits (1453 a 4), we must at the same time be able to identify ourselves with him. He is, as Aristotle asserts, a character "like" ourselves – not a god, angel, saint, or prophet. This transference of identity is in fact vital to the cathartic process. Under a hypnotic influence our old concept of ourselves is relinquished and we are induced to accept a higher one – a new identity. The effect is of course transitory. Every successful tragedy does not achieve the religious conversion of its audience, and as one of Plautus' characters remarks, "the audience applauds fine sentiments in the theatre, then goes home and proceeds to disregard them".[1] But it is hard to reject the conclusion that a re-orientation of the personality under hypnotism must predispose the mind to some similar change in real life.

In connexion with classical concepts of tragedy, Ibsen, of course, always creates problems. His characters are neither morally nor socially exalted, though they are sometimes intellectually superior. But the action which involves them is elevated at least to some extent through a didactic element and the sense that we are witnessing a "test case". The effect is, however, one of carefully calculated illusion, for as Mr E. M. Forster observes of Ibsen: "Although he is not a teacher he has the air of being one." [2] For some persons, the intellectualism of Ibsen's drama is enough to invest it with tragic dignity, for others it is not. The question is in fact one of degree; and in a border-line case tastes may be allowed to differ. Certainly there is nothing in Ibsen that proves Aristotle's prescriptions inadequate or too narrowly conceived. Aristotle makes full allowance for a didactic element in drama. Speeches should contain not only evidence of character but expressions of opinion (1450 a 6). Indeed, opinion is evidence of character, but since Aristotle specifies it as a distinct and separate element in drama, co-ordinate with Plot, Character, Language, Spectacle, and Music, we must infer that he attached to it some value of its own apart from mere evidence of character. What is even more important is his remark – to which we have already referred – that poetry (i.e. dramatic poetry) is "more exalted and more philosophical than history". It is so, he explains, because it deals with hypothetical instances of "probability and necessity", which, in so far as the poet is un-

---

[1] *Rudens*, Act 4, Sc. 7.
[2] *Abinger Harvest*, "Ibsen the Romantic".

committed to actual fact, permit him to deal with funda-
mentals – more in the manner of a philosopher. Necessity
also constitutes the principle which unites the beginning of
a story or dramatic plot to its middle and its middle to its
end (1450 b 26). It is inevitable that a work constituted on
such a "philosophic" basis should either pose a philosophic
question or offer a philosophic verdict. Yet it is interesting,
bearing in mind Mr E. M. Forster's shrewd comment on
Ibsen, to notice that the philosophy which Aristotle demanded of the dramatist was less real than apparent. This
becomes clear in the *Poetics* when we are told that in plot
construction a plausible impossibility is preferable to an
unconvincing possibility (1461 b 11). How Plato would have
frowned! Aristotle did not want the poet to be a real philosopher but merely to have the air of being one!

Furthermore, the formal arrangement of a well-con-
structed plot must in itself be reckoned a didactic element.
For form is memorable (1451 a 5) and what is memorable
is easily considered worth remembering. Again, the action
is dignified by our sense that it conveys a message, whether
or not it does so in actual fact. We should also notice that
the elements of surprise and detection (peripeteia and
anagnorisis, 1450 a 34), which Aristotle strongly recom-
mends to the poet are elements of dramatic form – part of
the plot construction. In the *Rhetoric* (1371 b) he states
clearly that such surprise elements, including "sudden es-
capes from danger", have an intellectual appeal like the
"syllogistic" process implied in the comparison of a picture
with the object which it represents. Indeed, dramatic surprise must follow the rules of probability and necessity
(*Poet.* 1452 a 20, 24), assisting in the tragic fall from fair to
foul fortune and in the involvement and denouement of the
plot. By the word "peripeteia", which we term a "surprise
element", Aristotle means an event which is forseeable –
inasmuch as it accords with probability and necessity – but
unforeseen by the audience. It is what the modern story-writer

calls a "twist", and its effect is to underline and emphasize whatever "philosophic" suggestions are present in the plot. Elements of surprise, as Aristotle tells us in the *Rhetoric*, inspire wonder, and the love of wonder as we may remember from the *Metaphysics* is closely allied to the love of wisdom.

All such didactic and philosophic elements, apart from the value of the lesson inculcated, tend to exalt the action, and in this connexion, perhaps, we should not be too eager to ridicule the neo-classic critics of the seventeenth and eighteenth centuries whose interpretation of Aristotle often seems so arbitrary. These critics had a taste for rules and therefore assumed more readily than they should have done that there were rules of taste. Yet their formalism had something of the Aristotelean spirit, and even the dramatic unities of time and place, which they deduced from Aristotle's ambiguous advice that dramatic action should be complete within a single revolution of the sun (1449 b 13), have something to recommend them whether they were propounded by Aristotle or not. Formality in construction suggests a seriousness of purpose and elevates the subject matter just as the artificial quality of metre elevates language. Of course, if everything is sacrificed to formality then the prevailing impression is simply one of artifice – but "abusus non tollit usum".

The last remark on elevated language brings us to yet one more aspect of that dignified concept of actuality which is an essential ingredient in the cathartic process as Aristotle saw it. Few critics would claim that the *Poetics* in the form in which it has survived is a well-balanced treatise, and despite the work done by modern scholars in clarifying the argument and ridding the text of interpolations, its purpose remains ambiguous and its structure correspondingly faulty. For this we must not blame the manuscripts but Aristotle himself. The treatise, as is claimed in the first sentence, is intended to be a comprehensive account of poetry, but it deals almost entirely with dramatic and epic poetry. The discussion of comedy remains no more than an unfulfilled promise, and to lyric poetry there is no allusion. It seems clear that Aristotle was distracted between writing an essay on poetry and composing an apology which would answer Plato's challenge as it had been formulated in the *Republic*. This would explain why mimesis, tragedy, and epic receive so much attention, although rhythm is recognized as a fundamental poetic instinct, and comedy, both in drama and narrative, is admitted to constitute a whole genre of poetic output. The fact is that mimesis, like tragedy and epic, had borne the brunt of Plato's attack, and hence these themes claimed Aristotle's attention almost exclusively in a work which was at least half intended as an apology. For the same reason, lyric poetry is not mentioned, since Plato had not attacked this genre – deeming that poetry in which the poet addressed the audience directly and not through the medium of characters was innocent.

These considerations partly explain Aristotle's indifference (in the *Poetics*) to questions of metre and rhythm. His statement to the effect that poetry is a matter of mimesis, not of metre (1447 b 15), seems hardly consonant with his other view that poetry springs at least in part from our fundamental susceptibility to rhythm – of which metre is an admitted aspect. Moreover, the well-known remark that the history of Herodotus would still be history, not poetry, even if it were written in verse (1451 b 2) is another example of overstatement on this subject. Aristotle's thought here seems unusually confused. The argument with which he supports his contention is that the poet is concerned with potentiality rather than fact, yet he himself neutralizes this argument not many lines later by the admission that potentiality may include fact. "There is no reason why fact should not conform to those principles of probability and necessity which are the poet's concern" (1451 b 30). Again, the example of Herodotus could hardly have been worse chosen. Herodotus had supplied more than one poet with material[1] and, for all the allegedly unphilosophical nature of history, furnished both Plato and Aristotle with allusions. It is, indeed, difficult to recall a historian who is more obviously delighted by "the wonderful"; and "the wonderful", according to Aristotle, is the basis of both poetic fascination and philosophic curiosity. It would seem that under the pretext of producing a thesis on poetry Aristotle is here also concerned to refute Plato's criticism. Plato had suggested that, stripped of metre, rhythm, and music, poetry had little to recommend it – "like handsome faces deprived of their youthful bloom" (*Rep.* 601 b). Aristotle in the controversial spirit of a debater undertakes to show that the opposite is true, and as often happens in controversy an overstatement on one side produces a corresponding overstatement on the other.

It is hard otherwise to understand why, in dealing with the elevating power of poetic language (1458 a 18), Aristotle makes no reference to rhythm or metre. In the *Rhetoric*, as we have seen, he recognizes rhythm and metre as a source of poetic exaltation (*Rhet.* 1408 b). In the *Poetics* all his comments on language are deliberately confined to style as determined by the selection of words, and except for a few remarks about the suitability of iambics to drama and hexameters to epic poetry, he studiously avoids all allusion to rhythm and metre. It is clear, however, that even within this narrow field of style, the presentation of an exalted actuality is considered to be the poet's object. Current or commonplace words make for clarity, but they are to be interspersed with a poetic vocabulary, notably with metaphoric and glossary words, which elevate the style. If metaphor and glossary are overdone they will pro-

---

[1] For the Greek dramatic version of Herodotus' Gyges story, see D. L. Page, *A New Chapter in the History of Greek Tragedy*, Cambridge, 1951.

duce "enigma and barbarism" respectively. Indeed, classical poetry, to an Englishman who is not in a position to appreciate its prosodic resources, may seem timid in its use of imagery, and there can be little doubt that an ancient Greek, uninitiated into our own poetic conventions, would have regarded a great deal of English poetry as "enigma and barbarism". The point, however, which we are trying to make is that, whether in the domain of prosody and style or of dramatic character and action, Aristotle proclaims the same tragic principle. Our common experience, even where this is in itself painful, must be elevated by association with other, more exalted elements. We are thus induced to accept tragic suffering for the sake of its dignity. In doing so we are temporarily reconciled to the worst that life can do to us, and this is the essence of poetic catharsis.

CHAPTER VIII

Comedy

Both in the *Poetics* and the *Politics* catharsis is associated with pity and fear – that is to say with tragic effect. It has often been suggested that Aristotle had in mind a corresponding comic cathartic theory which, if he indeed committed it to writing, has been lost. The other possible view is that comic literature and art depend for their effect on some other process not classifiable as cathartic. To this second opinion the present work subscribes. It is important to note that Aristotle did not regard comedy as determined by a "happy ending", although he considered the happy ending as appropriate to comedy. It is thus a comic characteristic, and yet not the essence of comedy. The essential difference between tragedy and comedy lies in the fact that the latter deals with humbler and meaner types of character. Thus at the beginning of the *Poetics* (1448 b 24) we are given an account of the origins of tragedy and comedy:

"Poetry soon branched in two directions in conformity with the respective dispositions of the poets. Serious writers portrayed lofty character and action; whereas those of coarser grain confined themselves to meaner instances. The result was satire in the latter case, as contrasted with hymns and occasional poetry in the former. We do not know of any such satiric poetry prior to Homer, but no doubt it existed in abundance. From Homer onwards we find plenty, and Homer himself provides an example in his *Margites* and other similar works. The metre associated with such compositions is now called 'iambic' because this word was originally indicative of the satire which men aimed at each other in iambic verse. The old poets were thus divided into composers of heroics and iambics. Homer's position among the serious poets was outstanding, not only because of the quality of his poetry but by reason of his skill in dramatic portrayal; and, what is more, he was the pioneer of true comic form, laughable rather than satiric. The *Margites* in fact bears the same relation towards comedy as the *Iliad* and *Odyssey* do towards tragedy. As tragic and comic drama emerged, poets were attracted in one direction or the other, whichever appealed to them more, and the epic poet yielded to the tragedian as the writer of satire did to the writer of comedy. For the dramatic form was superior and more dignified."

The preference for drama rather than epic would seem to be a question of Aristotle's personal predilection, but it is a preference which he bases on reasoned argument at the end of the *Poetics* (1462 a 5). He admits that the more popular tastes of a large theatre audience make for vulgarity, but blames the actor and musician for pandering to it – not the poet. More to the point is his argument concerning the size of the work. A play's extent is such that it conveniently accommodates a single dramatic action. An epic poet, however, in order to attain epic length is obliged to interweave more than one theme, with some inevitable loss to our sense of unity. The criticism, moreover, is wholly in the spirit of Aristotle's other observations on form and magnitude – which we have examined in an earlier chapter.

More interesting still is the distinction which Aristotle draws between comedy and satire. One could have wished to hear more of the subject. The word "satire" as we use it today seems a fitting translation for Aristotle's Greek (psogos), suggesting a work of irony, sarcasm, or invective, although the derivation of the word is of course Latin (lanx satur) and its meaning was originally simply "mixed dish" or "miscellany". Clearly, however, the difference between satire and comedy in Aristotle's view was that which exists between contemptuous and indulgent laughter.

K

The distinction often becomes very important. Thus in Mr T. S. Eliot's *Dialogue on Dramatic Poetry* one of the speakers remarks that Restoration Drama "assumes orthodox Christian morality, and laughs (in its comedy) at human nature for not living up to it". Yet this really begs the question. Is the laughter contemptuous or indulgent? Satiric or comic?

Returning again to the question of Greek comedy and "psogos", it is necessary to remind ourselves that when Aristotle speaks of comedy he has in mind the plays of fourth-century Athens, not the Old Comedy of Aristophanes which flourished in the second half of the fifth century. In the *Poetics* we read, apropos of the "philosophical" and hypothetical nature of poetry, that the poet merely "appends" names after composing his story. "This", continues Aristotle, "has become clear by now in comic practice; only when a convincing plot has been devised are names supplied for the characters, and these are such as may suggest themselves, not the names of individuals such as appear in the compositions of the 'iambic' poets". (1451 b 11) The "iambic" poets, as Aristotle explains in the passage previously quoted, were the satiric writers, the composers of "psogos". If the criterion is one of fictitious or actual names, then Aristophanes was a satirist, not a comic poet; for he raises his laughs at the expense of individuals such as Socrates and Cleon, and was not obliged to dissemble their identity by the use of fictitious names. But Aristotle probably regarded him as representing a half-way stage in the development from satire to comedy. This development Aristotle probably felt to be still continuing at the time of writing the *Poetics*, as is suggested by the expression "by now" in the above citation. Tragedy, we are told, developed through successive stages until it realized its full possibilities and so reached a point at which further development was not to be expected (1449 a 15), but the public encouragement of comedy was of comparatively late date (1449 b 1) and in Aristotle's opinion no doubt accounted for its more tardy evolution. For anyone trying to elucidate an Aristotelean comic theory, one depressing fact emerges from these considerations: not only are we deprived of all but casual allusions to the subject in Aristotle's own writings, but we have almost no extant examples of what he meant when he spoke of a comedy; for, apart from some important recent discoveries, fourth-century comedy has been entirely lost, and we rely mainly on the Latin imitations of Plautus and Terence for our knowledge of it.

However, Aristotle's stipulation that comedy deals with a meaner type of character is easy to appreciate. As to the question of the "happy ending" he tells us (*Poet.* 1453 a 30): "Second in order of merit comes that kind of (tragic) plot which some persons rate first. It contains a double theme, and is exemplified in the *Odyssey*, where the ultimate fate of the good characters differs diametrically from that allotted to the bad. It is rated first owing to the weakness of the audience, for the poets write in accordance with popular demand. The pleasure which it gives is that proper to comedy, not tragedy; for the deadly enemies in legend, such as Orestes and Aegisthus, ultimately leave the stage reconciled, and there is no killing or being killed." This accords very well with our own ideas, though, as we have said, it should be noted that the type of character, not the ending, is the prime determinant of comedy and tragedy in Aristotle's opinion.

Even if Aristotle never spoke or wrote at length on the subject of comedy, it is evident that he intended to do so and had in mind all the relevant material. The *Poetics* contains a well-known promise that he will deal with the subject after his treatment of hexameter verse (1449 b 21), but the *Poetics* has not survived in any document known to us beyond the discussion of epic poetry. The theory of comedy is missing. There is no agreement as to whether the *Poetics*

originally constituted two books, but it seems perfectly
clear that Aristotle's theory of comedy was quite accessible
to his contemporaries in some form or other. In the *Rhetoric*
(1372 a 1) we read: "Similarly, it follows that since amusement and all forms of relaxation, including laughter, are
enjoyable, the ridiculous, as exemplified in characters,
words, or deeds, will afford enjoyment. The ridiculous has
been separately classified in our treatise on poetry." Again,
in the same work (1419 b 5), Aristotle tells us: "The various
forms of the ridiculous have been enumerated in our treatise on poetry. Some may decently be employed by a person
of liberal education, others not. Care must be taken (by
the public speaker) as to the propriety of jest. Irony is more
appropriate to a person of liberal education than mere
clowning. The former jests for his private satisfaction, but
the clown is concerned with the effect that he will make on
others."

These passages also offer some clue as to the probable
contents of Aristotle's comic theory; and indeed if we ran-
sack the whole of Aristotle's writings for similar clues, a
formidable body of doctrine can be assembled. The task of
assembly was performed with great thoroughness by Lane
Cooper in a work published in 1922; and the resulting
accumulation may be supplemented, as it is in Lane
Cooper's work, by reference to Iamblichus, Proclus,
Tzetzes, the *Tractatus Coislinianus*, and other repositories of
Peripatetic tradition. At the same time, collections of comic
fragments such as those of Kaibel and Kock supplement
our pitifully deficient knowledge of Greek comedy in
practice.

As a result of this kind of research some of Aristotle's
commentators have come to believe in the existence of a
theory of comic catharsis. But we have already argued that
the notion of catharsis is not only purgative but purgatorial.
It is in fact expiatory, depending as it does on an acceptance
of suffering. The quality of tragedy, Aristotle maintains, is

determined by the subject-matter, and this is to be derived from the grim themes of Greek mythology, stories of fearful deeds and sufferings. Matricide is a particularly fruitful topic: the murder of Clytemnestra by Orestes, or of Eriphyle by Alcmaeon (1453 b 22). The best tragedies are all based on the old stories and the old heroes: Alcmaeon, Oedipus, Orestes, Meleager, Thyestes, and Telephus. We should not fail to observe that such stories are all accounts of expiation. The tragic hero commonly passes through "mania" to "purification", in which he rises superior to his suffering by accepting it.[1] The audience, who identify themselves with the tragic character, submit themselves to a similar process – experienced of course in a temporary manner through hypnotic suggestion. The point, however, which we are trying to make is this: Aristotle's view of catharsis in poetry and music is essentially expiatory, and it is impossible to associate comedy with any expiatory content.

Certainly, if we can arrive at any reasonable inference from Aristotle's own writings to the effect that the end of comedy was not conceived by him as cathartic, the explicit statements to the contrary in the *Tractatus Coislinianus* and Tzetzes are of so little authority that they do not even need to be explained away. The *Tractatus* is a tenth-century Byzantine manuscript dealing with poetic theory, and John Tzetzes was a scholarly commentator of the twelfth century. One has only to reflect on the modified form in which Aristotelean literary theory reached Horace to realize how little reliance can be placed on late Byzantine sources. In one respect, however, it would be wrong to disregard these accounts by which comedy is envisaged as "through pleasure and laughter effecting the purgation of the like emotions" or as "purgative of emotions, constructive of life, moulded by laughter and pleasure". At least, we should first examine the causes which led to such promulgations;

---

[1] In *Poetics*, 1455 b 15, the means of Orestes' salvation from "mania" is explicitly termed "catharsis".

for these may probably be detected in that isolated and precious statement on comedy which is preserved for us in our fragmentary version of Aristotle's *Poetics*:

"Comedy is, as we said, a portrayal of inferior characters. These, however, are not utterly wicked. On the contrary, the ridiculous is a species of ugliness. It is a kind of shortcoming, an ugliness which is neither painful nor deadly; and we may compare it with the comic mask, which, although somehow ugly and distorted, occasions no pain. The development of tragedy and the advances made by its successive exponents are on record, but the development of comedy, because it was not at first taken seriously, cannot be traced." (1449 a 32)

Now, it has often been remarked that such estimates of comedy as those of the *Tractatus* and Tzetzes' *Proem to Aristophanes* are based on the application of a mechanical substitution principle to Aristotle's famous definition of tragedy. It is a simple process of *mutatis mutandis*. Yet if we take the above passage from the *Poetics* into account such a process would not seem to deserve unqualified condemnation. Aristotle's statement on comedy bears a very clear antithetical relationship to his prescription for tragedy. In the first place we are told that comedy is a portrayal of inferior types. Tragedy, by contrast, presents more exalted characters (1454 a 16 etc.). Secondly, just as the comic character must not be wholly bad, so the tragic character must not be entirely good; it must contain a tragic shortcoming (hamartia). There even seems to be a terminological correspondence between the shortcoming (hamartema) which is the basic condition of comic character and that which, in tragic character, constitutes the one vulnerable point. It would be only natural to conclude that the "Achilles' heel" in the latter is matched by a "redeeming feature" in the former; and to these antitheses we may perhaps add that comedy is concerned with evils which are not deadly or fatally damaging, while pity, the tragic emotion, is roused by the prospect of just such fatal evils (*Rhet.* 1386 a 3). Comedy is concerned apparently with remediable as distinct from irremediable evils. The latter include death, injury, disease, hunger, and the various instances of ill-fortune which seem inseparable from human destiny. On the other hand, "remedies", as Aristotle observes elsewhere (*Rhet.* 1383 a 27), are a source of "confidence", and confidence is the opposite of fear. Such being the correspondence between Aristotle's surviving accounts of tragedy and comedy, it is not surprising that later commentators, even if they possessed no better documentary evidence than we do, were prepared to elaborate an antithesis of which Aristotle himself seemed so clearly aware.

However, a proposition may suggest more than one antithesis. Tragedy, we are given to understand, uses pity and fear to effect the catharsis of pity and fear. The proposition contains three factors. Firstly, there are emotions of pity and fear through which catharsis is effected. Secondly, there is the cathartic effect itself. Thirdly, there are the pre-existing emotions of pity and fear which are to receive treatment. On this basis, six different antitheses suggest themselves, and if we are to be guided only by our sense of antithesis, comedy may be defined in any one of the following ways, as (1) through pity and fear producing some (non-cathartic) effect on pity and fear, (2) through pity and fear effecting the catharsis of some other emotions, (3) through some other emotions effecting the catharsis of pity and fear, (4) through some other emotions producing some non-cathartic effect on pity and fear, (5) through some other emotions producing a cathartic effect on these same other emotions, (6) through pity and fear producing a non-cathartic effect on some other emotions.

Of these six speculative definitions, 1, 2, and 6 are hardly tolerable since the comic writer can in no sense be said to exploit pity and fear in producing his effects – though pity and fear may be regarded as emotions which his treatment is designed to combat. Number 5 is the definition offered in effect by the theorist of the *Tractatus Coislinianus*. It is unacceptable to us because the expiatory concept of catharsis at which we arrived does not seem congruous with the comic spirit. The same objection pertains to number 3. We admit no such thing as a comic catharsis. Only number 4, then, remains as a possible definition of comic effect: through some other emotions producing some non-cathartic effect on pity and fear.

What then are the other emotions, and what is the non-cathartic effect? The reference to pleasure and laughter in the *Tractatus* and in Tzetzes is obviously unsatisfactory, for pleasures are not, and were not regarded by Aristotle as emotions in the same sense as pity and fear. The analogy after which these definitions strive is thus forfeited. In the *Rhetoric* emotions capable of producing a change of opinion are listed as anger, pity, fear, and "all feelings of this sort" together with their contrary feelings (1378 a 24). Grief and pleasure are merely their concomitants. Now, if we are in pursuit of an antithesis and antithesis implies analogy, clearly we are bound to choose from the list of emotions analogous to pity and fear. Moreover, since contraries are included in this list, and since antithesis also implies contrariety, we shall naturally choose the contrary feelings of pity and fear. What are these? Aristotle himself tells us: "Indignation is the contrary of pity . . . envy also is contrary to pity, inasmuch as it is the same as or similar to indignation". (*Rhet.* 1386 b 10) Further on we read: "All such feelings (as indignation and envy) are an obstruction to pity, though they differ in the way described; and consequently they are all equally useful in preventing a feeling of pity". (1387 a 3) Of fear we are told in an earlier context: "Confidence is the opposite of fear". (1383 a 20)

In these observations it is possible to recognize the nature both of a non-cathartic comic process and of the emotions which it exploits in neutralizing the painful emotions of pity and fear. Thus we arrive at a comic definition which runs as follows: "Comedy is a portrayal etc. . . . through indignation and confidence effecting the obstruction of pity and fear." If Aristotle felt the antithesis between tragedy and comedy as acutely as his fragmentary remarks on comedy suggest, it is not unlikely that he somewhere committed himself to a formula of this purport. Where tragedy employs catharsis, comedy uses "obstruction" – or "colysis" if we must have a Greek word. Comedy repels fear by encouraging us; it repels pity, where this is excessive or misplaced (i.e. sentimental) by rousing a sense of indignation against such false claims on our sympathy. But this method is only successful where the objects of fear and pity are not the great irremediable evils of life. Where evil is of the "painful or deadly" kind, fear and sympathy have to be accepted, and the dramatic cure becomes homoeopathic, as in tragedy, not allopathic as in comedy.

It may reasonably be asked why we put forward indignation rather than envy as an emotion contrary to pity. Aristotle says that both indignation and envy are contraries to pity. He suggests, however, that envy is more selfish, being excited by those who are in competition with ourselves. Since the tragic emotion of pity is a sentiment and the emotion of fear an instinct – the first an unselfish, the second a selfish feeling – our sense of analogy should direct us towards the unselfish feeling of indignation when we are in search of pity's contrary and antidote. It is true that Plato, in the *Philebus*, had sourly identified the comic spirit with the feeling of envy, but that is no reason why Aristotle should have done so. On the contrary, it is rather a reason for Aristotle's not having done so! It is also worth observing that all effective dispositions of the human mind have their roots both in selfish and unselfish emotions. From the former they receive power, from the latter direction.

The comic definition on which we have speculated is certainly in accordance with observed psychology. For comedy is associated with laughter, and laughter arises from a sense of incongruity – of tension and relaxation, according to Bergson. In the comic sense we have a collision of painful with pleasurable feeling, such as does not occur in the tragic reaction – where pain is cured by pain. Even in the phenomenon of tickling two incongruent elements are present. Tickling is half way between an assault and a caress. It challenges and disarms us simultaneously. On the other hand, there is no absolute reason for associating tickling with comic feeling, just because our reaction is laughter in either case. Not only grief, but onions produce tears, and some psychologists have thought that tickling has a purely physiological explanation – among them Aristotle himself (*Problems* 965 a 23 and 904 b 22).

Whatever we decide about tickling, however, comedy clearly relies on our sense of incongruity, as for instance in bathos and sudden transitions from sublime to banal effect. It is interesting here to note the function of sublimity in comedy. If there were no place for it there would be no such thing as a comic poet. Every poet, as we have indicated, must possess the power to hypnotize. The tragic poet steadily tightens his grip upon the audience, but the comic poet wakens his victims as soon as they are entranced, drawing attention to the deceit which under his spell he has been able – or would have been able – to practise on them. For it is as easy to form false associations under the poetic hypnosis as it is to form authentic ones. Misplaced love, misplaced loyalty, misplaced enthusiasm are the counters with which the comic game is played, and if the comic poet is a true poet, not a mere humorist, we are allowed to feel the full force of such love, loyalty, or enthusiasm before being shown that it is misplaced. In real life, also, beauty entrances; and just as we must enlist its aid for the endurance of irremediable evil, so we must forswear its opium where a clear head is essential to our own interests and remedy lies in our own hands.

It would thus appear that although Aristotle means, when he speaks of tragedy and comedy, tragic and comic drama respectively, he recognized the tragic and comic attitudes as two fundamental differentiae pervading all literary and artistic composition. This being so, it naturally occurs to us to ask: did he not recognize an intermediate genre of tragi-comedy in which the tragic and comic attitudes were mixed and blended? In painting he did recognize precisely such a genre and we have already commented on the passage in which he compares three styles of painting: the ideal, the realistic, and the caricature. It is all the more surprising therefore to find that he makes no allowance for such an intermediate type of work in literature. English readers are familiar with the types of serious comedy or muted tragedy which in the plays of Shakespeare have sometimes been classified as "romances", and though such intermediate types are alien to the spirit of neo-classicism, they were by no means rare in the great body of Greek drama with which Aristotle himself was acquainted. The foremost experimentalist of Greek tragi-comedy was, of course, Euripides. The *Alcestis* is a tragi-comic fantasy; the *Iphigeneia in Tauris* an adventure story; the *Andromeda*, it would appear, was a love story. Sometimes the experiment was unsuccessful and produced a "confusion de genres" such as the *Andromache*. All these works were nominally tragedies, or, as in the case of the *Alcestis*, associated with a tragic trilogy. It is curious that Aristotle should have commended Euripides as the "most tragic" of the poets on account of the melancholy endings of many of his plays (1453 a 25) without apparently noticing that other so-called tragedies by Euripides had as much claim to be regarded as serious comedies. Nor is this a mere oversight on Aristotle's part He explicitly deprecates the type of plot exemplified in the *Odyssey*, in which vice is punished and virtue rewarded. Such an end, he tells us, is proper to comedy rather than tragedy; and his statement of course assumes that we have the right to judge the *Odyssey* by tragic standards. The truth is clearly otherwise. The *Odyssey* belongs to an intermediate genre in which both tragic and comic elements exist. Why Aristotle failed to recognize such intermediate status in poetry when he recognized it so clearly in painting is hard to understand.

Conclusion

Commentators on Aristotle's *Poetics* are frequently blamed for expounding what Aristotle should have said rather than what he actually did say; and in the present work I have been at absolutely no pains to escape the common reproach. This is because I believe that a commentator on Greek aesthetics is well employed in elaborating what Plato and Aristotle should have said. But be it immediately understood, this is not the same as elaborating what any writer on aesthetics should have said. It is not the same as attributing one's own view to somebody else. It is not the same as squaring Aristotle with one's own ideas, or justifying one's own critical theories by reference to Aristotle's authority. But in the course of the preceding chapters we have stated the view that it is the commentator's duty to assemble and systemize the scattered and unsystematic observations of the Greek philosophers on this subject. On retrospect we find the situation further complicated by the fact that both Plato in the *Republic* and Aristotle in the *Poetics* actually made abortive attempts at aesthetic systemization. These attempts, however, are in both cases undertaken partly in a polemical and contentious spirit and give little weight to many of the excellent observations which their authors made elsewhere. Indeed, both systems carry within themselves the seeds of their own destruction, or at any rate admissions which reveal their own incompleteness. Let us repeat then: the purpose of the commentator must be to systemize the incoherent but highly valuable observations of Plato and Aristotle on this subject, not merely reiterate the tenor of their own casual and prejudiced systems – in so far as they produced anything worthy of that name.

A theory assembled in this way from isolated observations has much to recommend it. It exhibits Plato and Aristotle as fundamentally united in the interpretation of aesthetic experience, and offers a solution to many of the problems which still occupy the minds of critics and aestheticians to-day. The basis of this Greek aesthetic is a dichotomy of experience into conscious and subconscious states. Conscious experience is compounded of rational and moral values; subconscious experience – available to us in hypnotic, i.e. half-sleeping or comotose states – is the realm of beauty and ugliness. Half sleep or imperfect sleep produces dream or nightmare, in which our delight or horror is disproportionate to waking values. Conversely, things which are formally beautiful or ugly when encountered in waking experience exercise a fascinating power; for that which focuses intellectual concentration, as we saw in our chapter on Rhythm, is in some sense hypnotic. There is no clear line of demarcation between the stimulation and the lulling of the intelligence. Awareness in one direction is achieved at the expense of abandon in another. Thus the approach to beauty may be subjective or objective, just as infection may be contracted by contact with outside infection or by the breakdown of internal resistance to it. Moreover the common use of the term "beauty" is confusing, because we use it to mean the "fascinating" as distinct from mere degrees of truth or goodness and at the same time to denote the truth and goodness which impinges upon the fascinating and so distinguishes it from ugliness. This was the point of our analogy of the pyramid in Chapter III.

Given the nature of beauty, it becomes possible to answer the aesthetician's further question – concerning the relation of life and art. We are confronted by a dilemma. If art is better than life, artists are better than the rest of us. If art is not better than life, then it is a mere distraction. Neither of these conclusions would recommend themselves to most of us, and the dilemma can only be avoided by affirming that art is *usually* but not *always* better than life. It is more than life in common actuality but less in potentiality. And here we may understand the sense in which Plato and Aristotle were complementary thinkers. Plato had found life greater and more inspiring than anything which art could produce, when he found it exemplified in the person of Socrates. Aristotle had had no such experience. On the contrary, Aristotle had been a pupil of Plato, and Plato was one of the greatest of literary artists. It is not surprising that one who was first drawn to philosophy by such a literary master should feel that life in actuality rarely rose to the dignity of life in literature and art.

The Greek aesthetic system as we have formulated it does not of course imply a set of rules by which art may be judged and the respective merits of different works and schools proclaimed. On the contrary, it affords clear evidence that no such rules are possible. Art makes moral and rational suggestions under a hypnotic spell. Its value depends no less on the moral and rational quality of the suggestions than on the efficacy of the spell. But morality and rationality may not be in direct proportion to each other, and although tragic art is mainly moral in tone and comic art rational, neither must actually do violence to the other's values. A question arises as to how far we may advance the interests of rationality without flouting moral standards or viceversa. All persons will not feel the same in individual instances. Again, rational and moral standards themselves differ with time and place. Furthermore, as regards hypnotic power, what fascinates one person will not necessarily fascinate another. This is merely a question of taste, and taste may be acquired where its acquisition is considered an advantage. But there is also good and bad taste – better and worse taste. Taste does not change only with time and place, but differs with the moral and rational standards of individuals. Certain types of fascination will be effective only when practised on persons of respectively higher or lower moral or rational standards. For instance, utterly uninstructed minds are not likely to appreciate formal beauty of any kind. Mediocre intelligences will appreciate only the more obvious kinds of formal beauty. Those who demand very abstruse forms are probably incapable of apprehending beauty through any but the formal medium and may well be in most cases morally insensitive.

Our conclusion must be that while certain works of representation and rhythm are in every respect superior and others are in every respect inferior, there is a wide range of material in which issues are so complex and equivocal that it is not possible to distribute praise or blame unreservedly. The social danger of evil and foolish suggestions made under surreptitious hypnotism is so great that the maintenance of a censorship is a measure well justified in most societies. At the same time, the fascination exercised by certain exalted works is of such obvious benefit that we rightly draw attention to them in the course of school and university instruction. On the other hand, there remains a vast corpus of intermediate work, brilliant and valuable in some respects, dangerous in others, on which it is hard to pronounce any clear judgement; for its effect will differ with time and place. Towards such work, which constitutes the greater part of artistic production, the State will be suspicious or sympathetic according to the prevailing ideology. On the one side, we have the attitude of Sparta, Nazi Germany, communist Russia; and on the other that of Athens and today's western democracies.

Bibliography

KEY TO BIBLIOGRAPHY

I. *Texts, Translations, and Commentaries*
   A. Opera Omnia
   B. Compilations, Assembled fragments, etc.
   C. Aristotle's Poetics
   D. Other works of Aristotle
   E. Works of Plato
   F. Other Authors

II. *Researches*

   A. Mimesis
   B. Catharsis
   C. Tragic "hamartia"
   D. Rhythm, metric and music
   E. Erotic idealism
   F. Comedy
   G. Aristotle in general
   H. Plato in general
   I. Aristotle and Plato
   J. Pre-Socratics
   K. Aspects of Greek Religion
   L. Greek Art and thought in general
   M. General Aesthetics

Note: Works of general philosophy or criticism have only been included in the Bibliography when they contain important allusions to Greek Aesthetic Theory or have a particular relevance to the argument.

Bibliography

The following publications have been taken into account in the course of the present work. For references to classical authors of whom no edition appears below the Teubner or Firmin-Didot series has generally been consulted.

I. Texts, Translations, and Commentaries

A. OPERA OMNIA

1. Burnet. *Platonis Opera*, recognovit brevique adnotatione critica instruxit Ioannes Burnet. 5 Tomi. Oxonii, 1905–13.
2. Firmin-Didot. *Aristotelis opera omnia graece et latine cum indice nominum et rerum.* Vols. I–V. Parisiis editoribus Firmin-Didot et sociis, 1927–31.
3. Jowett, B. *The Dialogues of Plato.* Translated into English with Analyses and Introductions. Revised by order of the Jowett copyright trustees. Oxford, 1953.
4. Ross, W. D. *The Works of Aristotle translated into English*, 12 vols. Oxford. Revised, 1949.

B. COMPILATIONS, ASSEMBLED FRAGMENTS, ETC.

1. Consbruch. *Hephaestionis Enchiridion* cum commentariis veteribus edidit Maximilianus Consbruch. Accedunt variae metricorum Graecorum reliquiae. mcmvi. Lipsiae in aedibus Teubneri.
2. Diels, H. *Die Fragmente der Vorsokratiker*, griechisch und deutsch: fünfte Auflage herausgegeben von W. Kranz. Berlin, 1934.
3. Kaibel, G. *Comicorum Fragmenta.* vol I. fasc. prior. Berlin, 1899.
4. Kock, T. *Comicorum Atticorum Fragmenta.* Leipzig, Teubner, 1884.
5. Westphal, Rudolf. *Die Fragmente und die Lehrsätze der Griechen Rhythmiker* von Rudolf Westphal. *Supplement zur Griechischen Rhythmik* von A. Rossbach. Leipzig. Druck und Verlag von B. G. Teubner, 1861.

C. ARISTOTLE'S POETICS

1. Butcher, S. H. *Aristotle's Theory of Poetry and Fine Art*. London. Macmillan (1894). Reprint, 1932.
2. Bywater, I. *Aristotle on the Art of Poetry*. Text, translation, and Commentary. Oxford. Clarendon, 1909.
3. Else, G. F. *Aristotle's Poetics. The Argument*. Harvard University Press, 1957.
4. Fyfe, W. Hamilton. *Aristotle's Art of Poetry*. Oxford. Clarendon, 1940.
5. Gudeman, Alfred. *Aristoteles.* Περὶ Ποιητικῆς, Mit Einleitung, Text und Adnotatio Critica, exegetischem Kommentar, kritischem Anhang und Indices Nominum, Rerum, Locorum. Berlin und Leipzig. Walter de Gruyter, 1934.
6. Margoliouth, D. S. *The Poetics of Aristotle*. Translated from Greek into English and from Arabic into Latin, with revised text, commentary, glossary, and onomasticon. London, 1911.
7. Montmollin, D. de. *La Poetique d'Aristote. Texte Primitif et additions ultérieures*. Neuchâtel, 1951.
8. Potts, L. J. *Aristotle on the Art of Fiction*. Cambridge, 1943.
9. Rostagni, Augusto. *Aristotele Poetica*. Introduzione Testo e Commento (1927). Seconda edizione riveduta. Bibilioteca di Filologia Classica. G. De Sanctis e A. Rostagni, 1945.
10. Sycoutris, J. Ἀριστοτέλους Περὶ Ποιητικῆς. Εἰσαγωγή, κείμενον καὶ ἑρμηνεία. (Μετάφρασις ὑπὸ Σ. Μενάρδου.) Ἀθῆνα, 1937.
11. Twining, Thomas. *Aristotle's Treatise on Poetry*. London, 1789.
12. Tyrwhitt, T. *De Poetica Liber*. Textum recensuit, versionem refinxit, et animadversionibus illustravit Thomas Tyrwhitt. Oxford, 1794.
13. Vahlen, Ioannes, *Aristotelis de Arte Poetica Liber*. Apud S. Hirzelium, Lipsae, 1885.
14. Valdimigli, M. *Aristotele Poetica*. Traduzione Note & Introduzione. Gius. Laterza & Figli. Bari, 1916.

D. OTHER WORKS OF ARISTOTLE

1. Barker, Ernest. *The Politics of Aristotle*. Translated with an introduction, notes, and appendices. Oxford, 1946.

2. Bywater, I. *Aristotelis Ethica Nicomachea*, recognovit brevique adnotatione critica instruxit I. Bywater. Oxonii e typographeo Clarendoniano, 1890.

3. Cope, E. M. *The Rhetoric of Aristotle*, with a commentary by the late E. M. Cope. Revised and edited for the syndics of the University Press by J. E. Sandys. 3 vols. Cambridge, 1877.

4. Freese, J. *Aristotle, The Art of Rhetoric*. Loeb Classical Library, 1947.

5. Joachim, H. H. *Nicomachean Ethics*, a commentary, edited by D. A. Rees. Oxford, 1951.

6. Rackham, H. *Aristotle's Politics*. Loeb Classical Library, 1950.

7. Ross, W. D. *Aristotle's Metaphysics*, text with introduction and commentary, 2 vols. Oxford, 1951.

E. WORKS OF PLATO

1. Adam, James. *The Republic of Plato*, edited with critical notes, commentary, and appendices. 2 vols. Cambridge. Reprint, 1926.

2. Burnet, J. *Plato's Phaedo*, edited with introduction and notes. Oxford. Clarendon (1911). Reprint, 1956.

3. England, E. B. *Laws of Plato*. Text and commentary. 2 vols. Manchester, 1921.

4. Hackforth, R. *Plato's Phaedrus*, translated with introduction. Commentary by R. Hackforth. Cambridge, 1952.

5. Hackforth, R. *Plato's Examination of Pleasure*. A translation of the Philebus, with Introduction and Commentary by R. Hackforth. Cambridge, 1945. Reprint, 1958.

6. Lamb, W. R. M. *Lysis, Symposium, Gorgias*. Loeb Classical Library, 1932.

7. Shorey, Paul, *Plato's Republic*. 2 vols. Loeb Classical Library, 1930.

F. OTHER AUTHORS

1. Festugière, A.-J. *Hippocrate. L'Ancienne Médecine*. Introduction Traduction et Commentaire. Paris. Libraire C. Klincksieck, 1948.

2. Hicks, R. D. *Diogenes Laertius*. Lives of Eminent Philosophers. 2 vols. Loeb Classical Library, 1950.

3. Immisch, O. *Gorgiae Helena* recognovit et interpretatus est Otto Immisch. Berlin und Leipzig. Walter de Gruyter, 1927.

4. Kroll, *Procli Diadochi in Platonis rem publicam commentarii.* Bibliotheca Scriptorum Graecorum et Romanorum Teubneriana, 1899.

5. Marchant, E. C. Xenophon, *Memorabilia and Oeconomicus.* Loeb Classical Library, 1953.

II. Researches

A. MIMESIS

1. Croissant, J. *Aristote et les Mystères.* Liège–Paris, 1932.
2. Koller, H. *Die Mimesis in der Antike. Nachahmung, Darstellung, Ausdruck.* Bernae Aedibus A. Francke, 1954.
3. Ransom, J. C. *The Mimetic Principle.* October 1935 issue of the *American Review,* New York.
4. Tate, J. *Imitation in Plato's Republic. Classical Quarterly,* 1928.
5. Tate, J. *Plato and Imitation. Classical Quarterly,* 1932.
6. Trench, W. F. *Mimesis in Aristotle's Poetics.* Hermathena 48, 1933.
7. Verdenius, W. *Mimesis.* Plato's doctrine of imitation and its meaning to us. Philosoph. Ant. III. Leiden. E. J. Brill, 1949.

B. CATHARSIS

1. Bernays, Jacob. *Zwei Abhandlungen über die Aristotelische Theorie des Drama.* (a) *Grundzüge der verlorenen Abhandlung des Aristoteles über Wirkung der Tragödie.* (b) *Erganzung zu Aristoteles Poetik.* Ein Brief an Leonhard Spengel über die tragische Katharsis bei Aristoteles.
2. Bignami, F. *La catarsi tragica in Aristotele.* Rivista di Filosophia neoscolastica 18, 1926.
3. Boekel, C. W. van. *Katharsis,* Een filologische reconstructie van de psychologie van Aristoteles omtrent het gevoelsleven. De Fontein. Utrecht, 1957.
4. Dirlmeier, F. Κάθαρσις Παθημάτων. Hermes, 1940.
5. Giesing, F. *Der Ausgang des Königs Oedipus von Sophokles und die Aristotelische Katharsis.* Commentationes Fleckeisianae. Leipzig, 1890.

6. Lorenz, E. *Ödipus auf Kolonos*. Imago 4 (1915–16).
7. Ransom, J. C. *The Cathartic Principle*. *The American Review*. New York, June, 1935.
8. Trench, W. F. *The Place of Katharsis in Aristotle's Aesthetics*. Hermathena 51, 1938.

C. TRAGIC "HAMARTIA"

1. Flickinger, M. K. *The ἁμαρτία of Sophocles' Antigone*. Iowa Studies in Classical Philology, No. 11. Iowa, 1935.
2. Glanville, I. M. *Tragic Error*. *Classical Quarterly*, 1949.
3. Harsh, Ph. W. *'Αμαρτία Again*. Transactions and Proceedings of the American Philological Association 86, 1945.

D. RHYTHM, METRIC AND MUSIC

1. Dale, A. M. *The Lyric Metres of Greek Drama*. Cambridge, 1948.
2. Georgiades, Thrasyboulos. *Der Griechische Rhythmus, Musik, Reigen, Vers und Sprache*. Marion von Shröder Verlag. Hamburg, 1949.
3. Gray, Cecil. *The History of Music*. London. Kegan Paul, Trench, Trubner & Co., 1928. 2nd ed. corrected and revised, 1931. Reprint, 1945.
4. Monro, D. B. *The Modes in Ancient Greek Music*. Oxford, 1894.
5. Shröder, Otto. 'Ρυθμός. Hermes, 1918.
6. Winnington Ingram, R. P. *Mode in Ancient Greek Music*. Cambridge, 1936.

E. EROTIC IDEALISM

1. Bowra, C. M. *Greek Lyric Poetry, from Alcman to Simonides*. Chapter V (Sappho). Oxford. Clarendon, 1936.
2. D'Arcy, M. C. (S.J.). *The Mind and Heart of Love*. A study of Eros and Agape. Faber & Faber, 1945.
3. De Rougemont, Denis. *Passion and Society*. Translated by Montgomery Belgion. Faber & Faber, 1956.
4. Lewis, C. S. *The Allegory of Love*. A study in medieval tradition. Oxford, 1936. Reprint with corrections, 1943, 1953.
5. Nygren, Anders. *Agape and Eros*. Christian Idea of Love. Translated by Hebert. S.P.C.K., 1932.

F. COMEDY

1. Bergson, H. *Le Rire*. Paris, 1900. Translated by Cloudesley Brereton and Fred. Rodwell as: *Laughter, an essay on the meaning of the Comic*. Macmillan, 1911.
2. Cooper, Lane. *An Aristotelian Theory of Comedy with an Adaptation of the Poetics and a translation of the Tractatus Coislinianus*. New York. Harcourt, Brace and Company, 1922.
3. Meredith, George. *An Essay on Comedy and the Uses of the Comic Spirit*. Ed. by Lane Cooper. New York, 1918.
4. Schmidt, J. *Euripides Verhältnis zu Komik und Komödie*. Grimma, 1905.
5. Starkie, W. J. M. *An Aristotelian Analysis of "the Comic"*. Illustrated from Aristophanes, Rabelais, Shakespeare, and Molière. Hermathena 42, 1920.
6. Wolf, A. *Laughter*. *Encyclopaedia Britannica*, 1956.

G. ARISTOTLE IN GENERAL

1. Armstrong, A. *Aristotle's Theory of Poetry*. Greece and Rome, 10, 1940.
2. Bignami, F. *La poetica di Aristotele e il concetto dell'arte presso gli antichi*. Firenze, 1932.
3. House, Humphrey. *Aristotle's Poetics*. A course of eight lectures. Revised with preface by C. Hardie. Hart-Davis. London, 1956.
4. Lessing, G. E. *Hamburgische Dramaturgie*. Herausgeg. und mit Einleitung begleitet von Georg Zimmerman, Berlin, 1873.
5. Lucas, F. L. *Tragedy in Relation to Aristotle's Poetics*. Hogarth. London, 1949.
6. Ross, W. D. *Aristotle*. Methuen. 5th ed., London, 1949.
7. Rostagni, Augusto. *Aristotele e Aristotelismo nella storia dell' Estetica*. Origini, significato svolgimenti della "Poetica". Studi Italiani di Filologia classica. Firenze, 1922.
8. Solmsen, F. *The Origins and Methods of Aristotle's Poetics*. *Classical Quarterly*, 1935.
9. Ulmer, Karl. *Wahrheit, Kunst und Natur bei Aristoteles*. Ein Beitrag zur Aufklärung der metaphysischen Herkunst der modernen Technik. Max Niemeyer Verlag. Tübigen, 1953.

H. PLATO IN GENERAL

1. Flashar, H. *Der Dialog Ion als Zeugnis platonischer Philosophie* (Dt. Akad. d. Wiss.). Berlin, 1958.
2. Hirzel, R. *De Bonis in Fine Philebi Enumeratis*. diss. Lipsiae, 1868.
3. Lodge, R. C. *Plato's Theory of Art*. International Library of Psychology, 1953.
4. Murphy, N. R. *The Interpretation of Plato's Republic*. Oxford, 1951.
5. Nettleship, R. L. *The Theory of Education in Plato's Republic* (1935). O.U.P., London. Geoffrey Cumberlege. Reprint, 1951.
6. Ross, W. D. *Plato's Theory of Ideas*. 2nd ed. Oxford, 1953.
7. Schul, Pierre-Maxime. *Platon et l'Art de son Temps (Arts Plastiques)*. Deuxième édition revue et augmentée. Presses universitaires de France. Paris, 1952.
8. Schweitzer, Bernhard. *Platon und die Bildende Kunst der Griechen*. Max Niemeyer Verlag. Tübigen, 1953.

I. ARISTOTLE AND PLATO

1. Finsler, G. *Platon und die Aristotelische Poetik*. Leipzig, 1900.
2. Werner, C. *Aristote et l'idéalisme platonicien*. Paris, 1910.

J. PRE-SOCRATICS

1. Burnet, J. *Early Greek Philosophy*. Black. London, 1892. Reprint, 1952.
2. Cornford, F. M. *Mysticism and Science in the Pythagorean Tradition. Classical Quarterly* xvi, 1922.
3. Howald, E. *Eine vorplatonische Kunsttheorie*. Hermes 54, 1923.

K. ASPECTS OF GREEK RELIGION

1. Dodds, E. R. *The Greeks and the Irrational*. Berkeley, 1951.
2. Guthrie, W. K. C. *Orpheus and Greek Religion, a study of the Orphic movement*. 2nd ed. revised. Methuen, 1952.
3. Jeanmaire, H. *Dionysos, Histoire du Culte de Bacchus*. Payot. Paris, 1951.
4. Parke, H. W., and Wormell. D. E. W. *The Delphic Oracle*. 2 vols. Blackwell. Oxford, 1956.

L. GREEK ART AND THOUGHT IN GENERAL

1. Atkins, J. W. H. *Literary Criticism in Antiquity.* 2 vols. Cambridge, 1934. Vol. I (Greek). Reprint, 1952.
2. Beazley, J. D. *Greek Art and Architecture.* Cambridge Ancient History. Vol. V, Ch. XV. (Sections i–vi by D. S. Robertson.) 4th impression, 1953.
3. Glotz, G. *The Greek City and its Institutions.* Translated by N. Mallinson. London. Kegan Paul, Trench, Trubner & Co. Ltd., 1929.
4. Gomperz, Theodor. *Greek Thinkers.* A History of Ancient Philosophy (1901). 4 vols. Vol. I translated by Laurie Magnus. Vols. I, II, IV translated by G. C. Berry. London. John Murray. Reprint, 1955.
5. Kitto, H. D. F. *Greek Tragedy; a literary study.* Methuen, 1940.
6. Page, D. L. *A New Chapter in the History of Greek Tragedy.* Cambridge, 1951.
7. Pickard-Cambridge, A. W. *Dithyramb, Tragedy and Comedy.* Oxford, 1927.
8. Pickard-Cambridge, A. W. *Dramatic Festivals.* Oxford, 1953.
9. Shepherd, J. T. *Attic Drama in the Fifth Century.* Cambridge Ancient History. Vol. V, Ch. V. 4th impression, 1953.
10. Sikes, E. E. *The Greek View of Poetry.* London. Methuen, 1931.

M. GENERAL AESTHETICS

1. Bosanquet, Bernard. *A History of Aesthetic.* Allen and Unwin. London, 1892. Reprint, 1949.
2. Carr, H. W. *The Philosophy of Benedetto Croce.* Macmillan, 1927.
3. Carritt, E. F. *The Theory of Beauty.* Methuen, 1949.
4. Collingwood, R. G. *The Principles of Art.* Oxford. Clarendon, 1938. Reprint, 1955.
5. Croce, Benedetto. *Estetica come scienza dell'espressione e linguistica generale. Teoria e Storia.* Quarta edizione riveduta. Bari, Gius. Laterza & Figli, 1912.
6. Croce, Benedetto. *Aesthetics. Encyclopaedia Britannica,* 1956.
7. Hegel, Georg Wilhelm Friedrich. *Vorlesungen über die Aesthetik.*

Mit einem Vorwort von Heinrich Gustav Hotho. 3 vols. Sämtliche Werke. Jubilaumsausgabe in zwanzig Bänden. Stuttgart, 1953.

8. Kant, I. *Critique of aesthetic judgment*. Translated by J. C. Meredith. Oxford, 1911.

9. Lucas, F. L. *Literature and Psychology*. Cassell, 1951.

Index

Abinger Harvest, 130 n.
Abu Bakr, 4
Achilles, 12, 95
Adam, James, 40
Adeimantus, 56
Aegisthus, 139
Agathon, 19–22, 46, 48, 60, 81
Alcestis, 147
Alcibiades, 20, 21, 23, 25, 49, 97
Alcmaeon, 141
Alice in Wonderland, 58
Andromache, 147
Andromeda, 147
Antigone, 129
Aphrodite, 46
Apollo, 47, 61
Apollodorus, 19
Apology, 58, 59, 82
Archilochus, 114
Ares, 28, 29
Aristides Quintilianus, 110
Aristodemus, 19, 21, 59
Aristophanes, 19, 21, 60, 138
Aristotle's Theory of Poetry and Fine Art, 104
Athena, 12, 47
Athene, 61
Athenian freedom, 80
Athens, 8, 20, 138, 152
Austen, Jane, 32, 33

Bacchants, 70, 72
Berdyaev, N., 16
Bergson, 7, 146
Bernays, 120, 125–7

Blom, Eric, 111 n.
Bosanquet, B., 13, 15, 44
Bosphorus, Greek view of, 115
Boswell, 4
Bowra, C. M., 46 n.
Butcher, S. H., 97, 104–6, 125, 126
Bywater, 128
Byzantine and Modern Greek, 111

Callicles, 56
Cephalus, 40
Chalchis, 71
Christian Trinitarian dogma, 4
Cicero, 66, 106
Cimon, 97
Classical Quarterly, 65
Cleon, 138
Clytemnestra, 141
Conrad, Joseph, 23
Coombes, H., 112 n.
Cooper, Lane, 140
Corneille, 129
Corybantes, 70, 72, 77, 127
Cretan prejudices, 80
Croce, 53
Cybele, 77
Cyrenaic philosophers, 87 n.

Dante, 31
Dante and Beatrice, 14
Delphic Oracle, The, 77 n.
Delphic priestess, 77
Democritus, 103, 110

De Mundo, 103
Dialogue on Dramatic Poetry, 138
Dialogues, 7, 16, 80, 84
Die Fragmente und die Lehrsätze der Griecheschen Rhythmiker, 111 n.
Die Mimesis in der Antike, 62 n., 108
Diogenes Laertius, 29 n.
Dionysius of Syracuse, 9, 106
Dionysius the First, 97
Dionysus, 58
Diotima, 22, 23
Dorian mode, 124

Elea, 45, 46
Eleusinian mystery rites, 123
Eliot, T. S., 18, 138
Empedocles, 45
Eriphyle, 141
Eryximachus, 19, 20, 44–46
Euripides, 69, 83, 104, 147
Evangelists, 4

First Alcibiades, 48
Forster, E. M., 130, 131
Francesca (di Rimini), 31
Freud, 31

Galen, 125
Glaucon, 56
Gorgias, 47, 48, 50, 56
Gorgias, 48
Greater Hippias, 47
Greek Lyric Poetry, 46 n.
Guinevere, 31
Gyges, 134 n.

Hackforth, Professor R., 16, 17
Hamlet, 95
Hector, 95
Hegel, 2, 106

Helen, 66
Hephaestus, 47
Heraclean stone, 70
Heracleitus, 44, 45, 103
Hermes, 114
Herodotus, 133, 134, 134 n.
Hesiod, 57, 78, 81
Hippias, 8–19, 25, 69
Hippias Major, 8–11, 29, 33, 38, 42, 43, 48, 88
Hippias Minor, 8
History of Aesthetic, A, 13 n.
Homer, in the *Republic*, 56, 57, 62; in the *Ion*, 69–74; in the *Symposium*, 78, 81, 82; criticized by Aristotle, 95; and satiric poetry, 136
Hopkins, G. M., 48
Horace, 141
House, Humphrey, 78

Iamblichus, 140
Ibsen, 130, 131
Iliad, 56, 95, 105, 137
Illyrians, 105
Imitation of Christ, The, 62
Inferno, 31 n.
Ion, attitude to poetry, 55; shortness of the dialogue, 68, 69; Socratic irony, 72, 73; comparison with *Laws*, 74–77; poetic inspiration, 81, 82; the hypnotic quality of poetry, 96
Ion, character and ability, 69; his discussion with Socrates, 70–74; devotion to Homer, 78; shortcomings as a critic, 82
Ionic dialect, 110
Iphigeneia in Tauris, 147
Isolda, 31
Ithaca, 95

Jowett, 31

Kaibel, 140
Keats, 43
Kock, 140
Koller, H., 62 n., 108
Koran, 4

Lancelot, 31
Lawrence, D. H., 7, 25
Laws, last of the dialogues, 3; songs without words, 38; chromatic music, 39; art and entertainment, 52; dialogue and dramatic form, 57; decadence of dithyramb, 59; cautious attitude to drama, 64, 68; comparison with *Ion*, 74–80; moral value of drama, 85; rhythm and harmony, 101; music, comparison with Aristotle's *Politics*, 124
Lectures on Aesthetics, 2
Leucippus, 110
Literature and Criticism in Writing, 112 n.
Longinus, 2
Lycurgus, 78–81
Lysias, 25

Macbeth, 20
Machiavelli, 5
Magnet, 69, 71
Mantinea, 22
Maracos of Syracuse, 98
Marchant, E. C., 47 n.
Margites, 136, 137
Meleager, 141
Memorabilia, 4, 47, 74, 88
Memorabilia and Oeconomicus, 47 n.

Metaphysics, Socratic logic, 11; mathematical beauty, 87; desire for knowledge, 91; wonder and mathematics, 95; the nature of philosophy, 107; rhythm and form, 110; form and magnitude, 114; wonder and wisdom, 132
Meteorologica, 103
Mimesis, 74 n.
Mohammed, 4
Musaeus, 71
Muse, 46, 70, 71, 75, 76
Muses, 61, 70–72, 74
Musical Companion, The, 111 n.

Nazi Germany, 152
New Chapter in the History of Greek Tragedy, A, 134 n.
Nicomachean Ethics, 87, 90, 91
Nietzsche, 53

Ocean, Greek view of, 115
Odysseus, 95
Odyssey, 56, 95, 137, 139, 147, 148
Oedipus, 129, 141
Orestes, 139, 141
Orpheus, 71
Orphic mystery rites, 123

Page, D. L., 134 n.
Paolo, 31
Parke, R. W., 77 n.
Parmenides, 6
Parrhasius, 88
Pausanias, 19, 46
Pauson, 106
Pericles, 97
Peripatetic tradition, 140
Persian kings, 121
Phaeacians, 95

Phaedo, 124

Phaedrus, 19

Phaedrus, comparison with *Symposium*, 17, 23–27; homosexuality, 28–31; romantic and intellectual beauty, 33, 36; juxtapositions in art, 41; beauty through sight, 43; deprecation of literary art, 55; assessment of human faculties, 64; poetic inspiration and "mania", 72, 76–79, 127

Pheidias, 12

Philebus, logical considerations, 6, 7; notions of beauty: apparent conflict, 16, 17; pleasures of eye and ear, 33; intellectual pleasure, 35; formal beauty, 38; mathematical pleasure, 39; comparison with *Republic*, 39–42; the sense of smell, 43; comparison with Aristotle, 87, 91; envy and comedy, 145

Phrygian mode, 124

Physics, 102, 103

Platon et l'Art de son Temps, 52

Plautus, 130, 139

Pliny, 66, 106

Plotinus, 2

Plutarch, 103

Poetics, Agathon as dramatist, 19; inspiration, 78; mutilated text, 83; dramatic poetry, 85, 86; size and order, 87; wonder, 94–96; the "ecstatic" temperament, 97–99; mimesis, two causes of poetry, 100–2; art and life, 104–9; dramatic form, 113, 114; progressive and inert arts, 116; catharsis, 119–21, 124, 127–9, 136; dramatic surprise, 131, 132; indifference to metre and rhythm, 133, 134; comparison with *Politics*, 136; origins of tragedy and comedy, 136; drama preferred to epic, 137; comedy and satire, 137; "psogos", 138; theory of comedy, 139, 140, 142; tragedy and expiation, 141 n.; commentators blamed, 149

Politics, proportion and harmony, 87 n., 88, 89; "enthusiasm", 98; art and education, 103; representations of character, 108, 109, 117; form, 112–14; catharsis in music, 119–22, 124; medical and religious catharsis, 123; catharsis, psychological questions, 126; comparison with *Poetics*, 136

Polus, 48, 49, 56

Polyeucte, 129

Polygnotus, 106

Problems, 87 n., 98, 146

Proclus, 55, 140

Proem to Aristophanes, 142

Protagoras, 10

Protagoras, 5, 8

Protarchus, 34, 35

Pythagoreans, 7, 13, 123

Quantum Theory, 7

Republic, justice debated, a logical device, 5; spasms, irrational and ugly, 30; comparison with the *Philebus*, 39–42; supremacy of the Good, 51 n.; art and beauty, 52–54, 88; denunciation of the arts, 55; justice in the State, 56; criticism of poetry, 57; dithyramb, 59; tragedy and comedy, comparison with *Symposium*, 59, 60; representational arts, 61; mimetic art, 62; good and bad art, 64–67; comparison with *Ion*, 68, 69; divinity free from falsehood, 75; poetry and music as "incantation", 77; poetry and education, 80; traditional classification of arts, 85; aesthetic values, comparison with Aristotle, 86, 107, 133, 134; music and gymnastics, 121; music, instruments and modes, 124; aesthetic system, 149

Restoration drama, 138

Rhetoric, functional beauty, 89; beauty and virtue, 91; types of mind, 97, 98; pleasure in portrayal, 102; rhythm and metre, 109, 110, 112, 116, 134; prose period, 113; dramatic surprise and detection, 131, 132; pleasure in the ridiculous, 140; comedy and remediable evil, 143; emotions and their contraries, 144

Rudens, 130 n.

Russia, 152

St. Paul, 4

Schuhl, Pierre-Maxime, 52

Sense and Sensibility, 32

Shakespeare, 147

Shaw, G. B., 10, 83

Shelley, 43

Shorey, 66

Shröder, Otto, 114

Simonides, 93

Socrates, in the dialogues, 3, 4; and Hippias, 8, 10–14, 69; function of the teacher, 9; at Agathon's party, 19–21; argues with Agathon, 21, 22; "revocation" in the *Phaedrus*, 25, 26; attitude to homosexuality, 31; on pure pleasure, 34–37; on formal beauty, 40, 41, 48, 49; on beauty and divinity, 46, 47; influence on Plato, 55, 120, 151; and Thrasymachus, 56; approaches politicians and poets, 58, 59; argues with Agathon and Aristophanes, 60; on representational art, 62, 63; considers the ideal State impracticable, 65, 66; on poetic inspiration, 68; and Ion, 69–74; distrusts the poet as critic, 82; on proportion in art, 88; the descendants of, 97; Aristotle's opinion of, 120; on catharsis, 123, 124; in Aristophanes' comedy, 138

Solon, 78, 79, 81

Sophist, 45, 46, 52, 53, 56

Sophocles, 104, 129

Sparta, 67, 80, 152

Spartan prejudices, 80

Spartans, 80, 121

Spirit and Reality, 16 n.

Statesman, 56

Symposium, romantic beauty, 17; a "cocktail-party", 18; story of, 19–24; compared with *Phaedrus*, 24–31, 33; Beauty, Goodness and Truth, 35, 48, 50; Beauty and sublimity, 36, 37, 40; harmony and rhythm, 44, 45; Beauty and harmony, 46; love of beauty in art and skill, 46, 47, 81; comedy and tragedy, 59, 60; Greek theatre audiences, 67; "daemons", 76; poetry and sublimated love, 78; poetry and Goodness, 79; Beauty and virtue, 90, 91; comparison with Aristotle, 94

Tate, Professor C., 65, 66
Telephus, 141
Terence, 139
Theaetetus, 56
Theory of Ideas, 6, 7, 11, 24, 62, 66, 108

Thrasymachus, 56
Thyestes, 129, 141
Topics, 87
Tractatus Coislinianus, 140–2, 144
Tristan, 31
Tynnichus, 71
Tzetzes, 140–2, 144

Utopian political systems, 80

Verdenius, W. J., 74 n.

Weil, 120
Westphal, Rudolf, 111 n.
Wormell, D. E. W., 77 n.

Xenophanes, 45, 104
Xenophon, 4, 47, 74, 88

Zeus, 28, 29, 47
Zeuxis, 66, 105, 106